TOGETHER

HOW HUSBAND & WIFE ENTREPRENEURS
BUILT A WINNING CULTURE

CHRISTI AND STEVE WADE

Testimonials For Together

Steve and Christi's journey is a worthwhile read on the importance of persistence, faith and culture. This book outlines learnings that will benefit all businesses and business leaders regardless of specialization. They candidly share the ups and down's and ways to overcome based on vision and purpose.

-Bill McBride President & CEO BMC3, LLC

I am so grateful I had the opportunity to begin my fitness career at Christi's. Steve and Christi recognized my passion and help me gain the confidence to take on multiple roles at the club. Now as a Fitness Director in the country club industry, I often find myself thinking "what would Steve and Christi do", especially when it comes to tough decisions or personnel issues. I've always marveled at how Christi would handle running the club and tending to her family while still taking time to be patient, present and authentic with staff and members. While I learned a lot about the fitness industry in my 4 years at Christi's. I also learned so much from Steve and Christi about the value of human connection and the importance of leading by example.

-Trish Boddy Director of Spa and Fitness Lost Tree Club – North Palm Beach, FL

"TOGETHER offers an insider's view of how to develop a thriving business, side by side with your spouse. Over a span of twenty years, Steve and Christi Wade combined forward-thinking ideas with hard work to achieve the American Dream. Getting there wasn't all roses and picnics. TOGETHER gives readers an honest look into the lives of a couple as they build their business - and their marriage - by choosing faith, respect, and gratitude as the core values of their personal and professional success."

-Ashley Barron, Author and Entrepreneur

Christi and Steve Wade/Together
Printed in the United States of America
Website: www.TogetherVB.com

Back Cover Photo by: Emily Walker

Together/ Christi and Steve Wade -- 1st ed.

ISBN 9798591546229 Print Edition

CONTENTS

To our children, Brenton and Jordan, who have made life an adventure; full of love, laughter, optimism, faith and a willingness to try new things.

Introduction

WHY AM I DOING THIS? STEVE'S STORY

I was thirty years old and recently married. My wife, Christi, was pregnant with our first child. I was working in my father's business, a company called Agritech Engineering. Our job was to help agricultural interests in areas of Africa, Asia, and Latin America install monorail systems for transporting produce. The job entailed a lot of travel from my home in Vero Beach, Florida, much of it to places that weren't particularly safe. I wasn't crazy about that aspect, and to be honest, the work was never my passion. But when I traveled, I made five hundred dollars a day, plus expenses. In 1990, that was great money.

We would use a hydraulic ram to tension a monofilament cable to 10,000 pounds of tension (i.e., five tons of tension). I was in Martinique, showing a couple of guys how to do this. They spoke Creole French, of which I had only a rudimentary understanding, so my instruction was mostly via hand motions.

I was telling a guy to hold one particular piece of cable down to another to keep it out of the way, so I could create tension with the hydraulic ram. Suddenly, the cable slipped out of his hand and caught me right between the eyes.

There I was, in the middle of nowhere—on a banana farm in Martinique, of all places—with blood pouring off my face and streaming down my shirt. I could feel the blood, but I had no way of looking at myself to see how bad it might be.

I turned to the guys, hoping for some kind of reaction from them. One of them said, "*Pas grave*," which means "not bad" in Creole French. But my shirt was covered in blood, and I wasn't exactly trusting these guys. I didn't know if their idea of "not bad" was anything like mine. For all I knew, as long as you're not losing a limb, maybe your injury is "*pas grave*."

I started running toward my truck, which had a side mirror. It was about five hundred yards away. As I ran, I could feel my blood pressure rising. The blood from my injured face was really flowing now, and by the time I got to the mirror, I could see that my entire face was covered with blood, and I had an opening in my forehead that clearly would need stitches.

But it was Sunday, and in Martinique, hospitals are closed on Sundays.

The guy who'd dropped the cable said to me, "I have a doctor."

I let them drive me to a nearby house. It was made of bare cement walls and it was markedly unclean. But what choice did I have?

So there I was, lying on my back on a wooden table, having some guy stitch up my face in his house. I looked up at the ceiling, seeing cobwebs and spiders.

I can't believe I'm getting stitched up here, I thought. *I just want to be back in the good old U.S. of A.*

Later that night, back at my lodging, I lay awake in the dark.

How did I get here? I wondered. *Why am I doing a such a risky job, especially when I have no real passion for it?*

In the following days, these questions became louder in my head, as I finished that job and boarded a plane for home. I found myself asking God for answers—and I believe He delivered.

LET'S TALK ABOUT IT: CHRISTI'S STORY

As soon as Steve got home, we began to discuss it. What were our options? How could we make a viable income, be there for each other and our soon-to-be-born child, and be engaged in work that fulfilled us?

We were both passionate about fitness. I was directing a successful group exercise program at a local health club and had eleven years of experience in the industry. Steve had always loved working out and staying fit.

And clearly, he didn't want to travel as much for work. Prior to our having children, Steve's travel wasn't a huge deal. Depending on my schedule and where he went, sometimes I would fly out to meet him for a week. But we knew that with starting a family, we wanted to be more grounded in Vero Beach.

Could we combine those two things: our love of fitness and our desire to own a thriving business, one that was valued within our community?

Answering those questions formed the start of an incredible journey, one that stretched us as professionals, as individuals, and as a couple. This journey, which eventually led us to becoming a successful husband-and-wife business team, also provided incredible rewards—financially, yes, but (perhaps more importantly) also in the form of treasured friendships and community relationships.

WHAT THIS BOOK IS ABOUT

This book tells the story of that journey. It explains the ups and downs of our early years in business, the pitfalls we encountered and how we climbed out of them, the strategies we used to expand our business, and how we eventually found ourselves ready to sell the business and move on to the next phase of our lives. At the same time, we'll talk about how our faith, especially the message of "Do unto others as you would have them do unto you," helped shape every personal and business decision we made.

In this book, you'll find advice about starting a business, as well as how the decision to do so can affect your personal life. You'll learn how to capitalize on your business's highs and weather its lows. You'll see that many potential pitfalls can be avoided when your attitude is positive and your heart is truly in the right place.

HOW TO READ THIS BOOK

Together: How Husband & Wife Entrepreneurs Built a Winning Culture is primarily chronological. We'll start by explaining our histories, both individually and as a couple. We'll talk about the 1997 founding of our business, which we initially called Christi's Fitness and Weight Management. We'll discuss the early years, the middle years (when we became Christi's Family Fitness), and the later years, up to and including the 2018 sale of Christi's Fitness (the final name of the company, still in use today by its new owners).

At times, we'll break into certain key areas (such as discussing staff and member relationships) or significant events in our family life that both affected us personally and influenced how we worked together as business partners.

Concluding each chapter, you'll find a list (titled "Elevate the Ordinary") of strategic takeaways that you can use as you consider starting a journey toward business ownership, as well as concepts to apply as your business grows.

We hope you find this book helpful and inspiring. We look forward to sharing our journey with you!

CHAPTER ONE

HOW DID WE GET HERE?
AND WHERE DO WE GO NOW?

CHRISTI'S ADOPTION STORY

This story begins with a young Air Force pilot named John and his wife, Lenore. Early in their marriage, John and Lenore had a son, Mark. They planned to have more children—but as we all know, things don't always go as planned.

Four years passed without Lenore conceiving another child. At that point, John and Lenore figured it wasn't meant to be. They decided to adopt.

Not long after they made that decision, John was sent to Vietnam. While there, he flew over one hundred reconnaissance missions. After an area was bombed, he'd fly in with a photographer to capture images of the destruction. That was one dangerous job; they were sitting ducks for ground-to-air missiles, and they were unarmed when they went in. John lost many friends among his fellow pilots and photographers. Every day, he feared for his life, but he had a job to do, and he did it bravely.

Meanwhile, Lenore was back home in Tampa, raising a young child alone. One day, she got a call letting her know a baby boy was available for adoption. But she didn't know when (or worse, if)

John would return. Can you imagine her conflicted feelings? I'm sure it was agony, but Lenore said no, putting the idea of adoption on hold.

As it turned out, John was one of the lucky ones who made it home from Vietnam. God must have been watching out for him. And His plan for John and his family became part of the plan for me, too. Almost immediately after John returned to the U.S., he and Lenore learned that a baby girl was available for adoption.

This time they said yes, and yours truly joined the family as an infant. They named me Christina, calling me Christi for short.

Things got even better, though. To their surprise and delight, John and Lenore had another biological child—my sister, Karla, who was born two years later. It was such a blessing to have a sister I could grow up with and grow close to.

GROUNDED

When my siblings and I were young, our mother, Lenore, was a stay-at-home mom. After his active military service, our dad, John, went into the Reserves and worked as a commercial pilot. He flew for Braniff International, and he was with them when they went bankrupt. Karla and I were in high school then, and Mark was in college. I'll never forget that day. Dad was in South America when it happened, and we were shocked when he walked in the door. But all the crews had simply been told to get on flights and go home.

Dad took a job as a pilot for a cargo airline. But he didn't care for it, so he went back to school to work on his master's degree. He became a middle school science and math teacher. To make ends meet, Mom worked full time at a law firm in downtown Miami, as a secretary.

After a while, Dad left teaching and took a job with the FAA, both because he missed the world of flight and because it allowed Mom to work less. In retirement, Dad did consultation work for various airlines and flight-related organizations.

As my parents went through all these changes, their commitment to one another and our family was unwavering. I was a typical teen, more interested in my own life than my parents', but looking back now, I see two people who were grounded, resilient and devoted to their very cores.

POWERFUL EXAMPLES

While my parents made sure our home life was relatively calm and stable, they also insisted on a lot of movement and activity in our day-to-day lives. (Maybe that's *why* our home life was calm and stable!)

All of us were involved in activities. "I don't care what it is," Dad would say, "but everybody does *something*."

Dad enjoyed running, tennis, and fishing. Karla was into horseback riding and showing horses. Mark was an avid runner and fisherman. As for me, when I was little, swimming was my thing. We lived on a big lake, and we all learned to swim when we were small. By my early years of elementary school, I was swimming competitively.

Around third or fourth grade, a friend invited me to go to gymnastics class with her. From the start, I was hooked. I loved how gymnastics made me feel: agile, strong, and self-confident. I'd have happily kept doing both sports, but my parents wanted me to choose between competitive swimming and gymnastics. They knew that trying to do too much as I got older would prove difficult. I went with gymnastics.

While encouraging an active lifestyle, my parents also made it clear that school was important. My siblings and I attended a private Christian school. Mom helped in the school library and as the guidance counselor's secretary, giving us a discount on tuition.

In our home, there was an emphasis on family unity. Dad's way of connecting was through projects and travel. On the weekends, you'd find us all out in the yard, working together on some project. Because he was a pilot, we took at least one adventurous family trip each year.

My mom is an ultra-nurturer. I've never met anyone who doesn't love her. Dad is all about integrity, honesty, and doing the right thing. Their personalities worked together to create a powerful model of partnership and equilibrium.

LEARNING BALANCE: HIGH SCHOOL GYMNASTICS

In high school, I fully committed myself to gymnastics. Club gymnastics can be grueling; few gymnasts make it all the way through their senior year of high school doing club. It demands a lot of time, and many coaches are strict, especially at the higher levels.

I was fortunate to have had a coach who understood balance. He'd tell us, "You don't have to miss your other extracurricular activities to be on this team."

I wanted to be a cheerleader, which I saw as a natural fit, with all the flipping I could do. It also would give me more social time with my peers. My coach was all for it. He said, "If you have to miss gymnastics practice here and there, and then run over and jump in, great."

That was another good life lesson. Years later, this philosophy is something I incorporated into the children's programs at our gym. I didn't want our activities to put pressure on kids. I wanted them to *enjoy* being physical, because I knew that if they enjoyed themselves, they'd keep at it.

During my junior year, I almost left gymnastics. I confessed to my coach and my mom that I was burning out. Around then, USA Gymnastics (the national governing body for gymnastics) altered their event structure. So, my coach did a little shift in our system. Previously, I'd had to complete eight routines, but that year, it changed to four. As a result, I stuck with it. That was another valuable lesson about balance.

FINDING MY NICHE

I got a scholarship to the University of Maryland, Baltimore County, a Division II school. I enjoyed it, especially being on the gymnastics team, but I wanted to explore something else. And I missed Florida! My sophomore year, I transferred to the University of Florida in Gainesville.

While I was in Baltimore, one of the seniors on the team did an internship in Exercise Physiology. That caught my attention, and I became interested in this field. When I transferred to Florida, I described what she was doing in her degree, and asked to be pointed in the right direction.

I ended up majoring in Exercise and Sports Sciences. (Some universities call it Exercise Physiology or Kinesiology.) I liked the anatomy and physiology part; I was fascinated to learn how the human body moves. I didn't care for the more abstract scientific aspects, like the biology or chemistry. I liked the hands-on part of it.

In Gainesville, I worked a couple of part-time jobs. One was coaching at Sun Country Gymnastics. That was a job I went to eagerly, because it allowed me to help children learn the sport I loved. Gymnastics had taught me so many valuable life lessons, as well as giving me an edge when participating in other sports.

I realized my athleticism and artistry would be an asset in pursuing group exercise opportunities. I started teaching group exercise at a local gym, venturing into the fitness industry. Years later, Steve said all of this made it easy to choose the name for our health club: Christi's Fitness.

STEVE - LEADING BY EXAMPLE

Evenings, when I was growing up in Scituate, Massachusetts, my family always knew where to find Dad: in the basement, lifting weights in his underground home gym. He also commuted by bicycle twenty-six miles each way to his job in Boston. This was in the early 1970s, when most dads were driving gas-guzzlers to work and riding the couch at night. My dad was definitely unusual, but you had to admire the guy.

Dad's routines gave him a sense of independence and adventure. I think that's why he had such a positive attitude. Those habits also kept him fit well into his eighties. (I'd guess many of those couch-riding dads didn't fare quite as well.)

My dad led by example. He never told my four siblings and me to run, lift weights, cycle, swim, or do anything else active. But watching him all those years spoke loudly to us. All five of us adopted healthy lifestyles and incorporated fitness into our lives. This was a lesson I later modeled for my own kids—and, being a health club owner, I led by example for my employees, too.

Dad was also skilled in carpentry and very handy around the house. He didn't formally teach me these skills, but he was always happy to let me watch and learn. Those lessons, too, proved to be critical to Christi's and my business, in the years to come.

ANOTHER JOB WELL DONE

My first job was at a convenience store, stocking shelves and running the register. It was great having extra spending money, but what I really loved was the independence and sense of responsibility I received from working. I didn't just punch in my time card, go through the motions, and punch out every day. Instead, I embraced my job.

Maybe I was destined to be a business owner, because there I was, a teenager, considering how I'd want the store to look if it were mine. I made sure every product was lined up on the shelf with its label facing out. When I stocked milk in the cooler, I wiped off any condensation or dried milk before each container went in. After a customer bought a gallon of milk, I went to the cooler and pulled the next gallon to the front.

I loved the concept of everything being done right. When I cleaned, I cleaned thoroughly. I found it was easier to maintain cleanliness when I stayed on top of it, instead of letting grime accumulate.

If you asked my boss from those days, he'd probably say, "Yeah, that Wade kid had a great work ethic." I guess that's true, but for me it was just doing it right.

In retrospect, it was probably perfectionism in its infancy. As I got older, this trait showed up again and again. When I worked in construction, something was level only if the bubble was *exactly* between the two lines on the level. Paint had to be applied so that there were no missed spots. Clean meant *clean*—immaculately clean.

My dad had given me a great example to learn from. Even though he is now deceased, I can still hear his voice echo in my head saying, "Another job well done." Words he often used for his own work.

ACADEMIC HONESTY – A FORK IN THE ROAD

Following high school, I went to community college, and after a couple of years I transferred to the University of Florida. I loved computers, so I decided to go into computer science. I'd done some programming language classes in community college, and I was excited to take programming courses at UF.

One of my first programming classes was nicknamed the "weed-out class." In other words, if you couldn't hack it in that class, you were not destined to get your computer science degree.

This was in the days of Fortran and Cobol. Your finished program for each assignment had to be exactly like everyone else's. It wasn't like writing an academic paper, where nuances in what you said and how you organized the information could affect your grade. With writing code, there was only one right answer, and the code for that answer had to be written in a certain way. That meant when one student got it, that student could, in theory, give the answer to everyone else.

To minimize this problem, we had to sign a document called the Academic Honesty Statement. It said you promised you wouldn't go to any of the other students in the class for "help" with assignments.

Confession: my morals at that time were not great. I was kind of a partier, and I was all over the map. But my friends in the class had signed the Academic Honesty Statement, too, and even if I didn't take the document seriously, they did. As a result, I couldn't ask them for help.

You might wonder why I didn't use a tutor. Believe me, I tried. I'd go into these big labs and there'd be one tutor for forty students. I'd wait around, get stuck—and even if I got to spend a few minutes with the tutor, I left with no understanding of what I was doing wrong. Talk about frustrating!

I'm sure you can guess what happened. I was quickly "weeded out." I dropped the programming class and dropped out of the computer science major.

This is so unfair, I thought. *I want to get help and succeed in this class, but clearly that isn't going to happen.*

I was disappointed not in myself, but in the system. Here I was playing by the rules, acting with integrity, and it felt like I'd been given a raw deal.

But now, looking back, I see how that experience actually steered my life in a great direction. We probably all remember parents and teachers saying things like, "There's a light at the end of the tunnel." No college kid wants to hear that, but it really is true. It's just extremely difficult to see it while we're going through tough times.

Looking at the credits I already had, and trying to be practical, I switched majors to Business Management. Over time, as I learned about management, my skill set began to develop. Years later, when Christi and I were running our business, I did a lot of the hiring and firing. I ran an inclusive management program. I wanted to help my employees be "people-people." I didn't care if they could write a computer program, but I sure wanted them to know how to build relationships.

THE ONE

When we wrote this book together, we each had an opportunity to tell this story. We decided to recount both versions here.

Christi's Version: We met at the University of Florida. We were at a party, and we had mutual friends. Steve came up to me when I was by myself and struck up a conversation. I don't remember what he said initially, but it wasn't long before he told me, "I'd really like to go out with you."

"I can't," I replied. "I'm here with a boyfriend."

That was that. We both moved on.

Then, about six months later, one day I was walking on campus. By then, I'd broken up with the guy I'd been with at the party. Completely out of the blue, Steve and I ran into each other.

"Hey," I said, "is the invitation still open?"

He said yes. We played tennis on our first date. Tennis was his thing, but I hung in there, so we had a great time!

Steve's Version: I had a couple of dorm friends that knew people at her apartment complex. One day when we were over there, I saw Christi. I was really drawn to her, but I didn't know how to approach her, and I heard she had a boyfriend.

That same night, I saw her at a party. I figured it was now or never. I remember leaning over and saying in her ear, "Just go out with me one time. Just once."

I was disappointed when she said no—and ecstatic when, a few months later, she said yes. And I was impressed by her tennis skills!

Both of Us: We began dating, and we've been together since. We got engaged four years after we met.

Steve said then (and still says now), "I'd never before met anyone with Christi's combination of inner and outer beauty. Finding such a balanced person with a consistently upbeat attitude was rare. I knew she was special."

About Steve, Christi says, "He's always had such a positive attitude. He's sensitive, spontaneous, and fun. From the start, I loved that he was up for doing anything...as long as heights aren't involved! Steve has never been a fan of heights."

THE REAL WORLD

Our last few years of college went quickly. We both enjoyed our majors. We loved being together, and our relationship became serious. Not long after Steve's graduation, we got engaged. Like any newly engaged couple, we were excited for our future. But we also knew that the "real world" would soon loom large in our lives.

Just Get a Job – Steve's Story: I graduated a semester before Christi and began job hunting. My degree was in Business Administration Management. My opportunities upon graduation in 1988 were mostly "manager-in-training" jobs. That was code for floor-sales positions, making about $25,000 per year. I wasn't interested in that line of work, and I kept looking.

Eventually, I took a job at Ford Motor Credit. It was okay, nothing great. Just a job.

One day, when I'd been on the job for about three months, my dad called. "See if you can take a leave of absence," he said. "I have an opportunity for you."

My father had worked for thirty-five years as a civil engineer for United Brands International, the parent company behind Chiquita Bananas. Now retired from United Brands, he was establishing his own consulting engineering firm.

He'd gotten a lot of work right away, unusual for a start-up company, but there was huge demand for his services. He needed help with this new venture. I asked my boss at Ford Motor Credit if I could take a leave, and he said yes.

My dad told me I'd make five hundred dollars per day, plus expenses. Talk about appealing! I had dollar signs in my eyes.

I learned about the not-so-appealing aspects of traveling to remote locations later: malaria pills, yellow fever shots, the threat of AIDS. Oh, and how can I forget the lack of hot water and air conditioning? And the village generators, which turned off at 7:30 every night? Still, after a long day on the banana farms of the Ivory Coast in Africa, returning to the village where I was staying was a welcome sight.

My dad wanted Christi and me to move closer to him. He was in Sebastian, Florida, slightly south of Melbourne. Christi and I decided that after we got married, we'd move to the Melbourne area.

I thought working for my dad would be temporary, but I ended up staying for eight years. Eventually I took over his company,

Agritech. I traveled all over the world. As I mentioned in the introduction to this book, it was a great way for me to make a living—for a number of years, anyway.

It was great…until it wasn't.

Getting Started in the Fitness Industry – Christi's Story: After graduation from UF, I interned at the Doral Saturnia Spa in Miami, which, at the time, was one of the hottest spas. They'd opened two years earlier, after the company did a $42 million renovation. All the rich and famous people were going to Doral Saturnia. I was given a $100 tip on my first week there, which was pretty exciting!

Beyond that, it was an educational internship. I worked under the exercise physiologist, doing submaximal stress testing and body fat testing, and putting people in exercise programs. My supervisor was hands-on. She was phenomenal.

"Negativity is like a cancer, left untreated it can spread."
– Steve Wade

First Management Lesson: One day, one of my managers at Doral, Kathy Sanders, called me into her office. She sat me down and said, "I was in the cafeteria the other day and I heard everyone talking negatively about the policy of 'no dates' for the holiday party."

I nodded. I'd been there, too. In fact, I'd been sitting at the table where that conversation took place.

Kathy went on, "Christi, I don't want you getting wrapped up in that sort of thing. I see management potential in you—and as a manager, you can't get involved in the gossip. Or any of the stuff at lower levels."

She stopped speaking, waiting for my reaction. What could I say? I was stunned. I could feel my face redden with embarrassment.

Kathy softened and told me it was okay. "You're learning, Christi. I see you learning from your mistakes, and that's a great skill. A vital management skill."

This incident spoke loudly to me. There'd been about eighteen people at the cafeteria table where I was sitting. That Kathy singled me out was impactful, especially when I realized she singled me out not to reprimand me, but to mentor me.

I've shared this story multiple times throughout the years with people who worked for us at Christi's Fitness. If I saw someone who I thought had leadership traits getting caught up in gossip, I tried to help them rise above it and not get mired down.

Building a Career: During my internship, my supervisor started working part time at Doctor's Hospital in Miami, and she brought me on part time there, too. At Doctor's, I did work with their prenatal program. During this time, I also did corporate fitness for *The Miami Herald*, at their facility for employees.

After I finished my internship at Doral, I was hired on full time by them as an assistant. Not long afterward, my boss there decided to move on full time with Doctor's Hospital. She needed to hire a lead exercise physiologist to replace herself at Doral. They went through several interviews, thinking they'd get someone with a master's degree. But they ended up coming back to me, because I'd interned there, and offered me the lead position. I continued with

Doctor's Hospital and *The Miami Herald* part time. So, I had my hands full working—and planning our wedding.

Following the wedding, we moved to Melbourne. I began doing in-home personal training, as well training in a few clubs around town. I also began working for the Athletics and Fitness Association of America (AFAA) as a consultant. On weekends, I'd travel around the country, training new group exercise instructors. About a year later, one of the clubs I did a little personal training for wanted to start a group exercise program, and they asked me to manage it.

Steve was traveling for his dad's company, so we were busy and on the go all the time. But we were young, childless, and having fun. We were making good money, traveling, and (for me, anyway) engaged in gratifying work.

Not long afterward, we moved to Vero Beach, to be closer to Agritech's base office. Steve had a business partner, and his partner's wife, Jill, was a group exercise instructor in Vero Beach.

"Let me take you around," she said to me. "I'll introduce you to the club owners in town."

I happily took her up on that—and, as a side note, when we opened Christi's Fitness, Jill became one of our first instructors. She ended up teaching for us all twenty-one years we owned the business.

Within a few months, a husband-and-wife business team reached out to me. They asked me to come on board when they opened a World Gym in Vero Beach. I spent the next couple of years helping to run their group exercise programs.

About those years and the career I was building, Steve has this to say: "In an industry where some class instructors wanted the best time slots and the fullest classes in order to 'perform,' Christi stood out as a humble, servant leader. She didn't always take the most popular time slots for her classes. She mentored her team of instructors. Her constructive feedback and praise stood out as unique among other health-club group exercise directors. She cared enough to spend time with people to enhance their abilities. More than what she said, it was her actions that inspired employees and members to enjoy fitness. A genuine, serving heart is the biggest differentiator any business can have, and Christi has always had that."

THE DECISION TO SHIFT GEARS

After the birth of our son, Brenton, we began talking about starting a business in Vero Beach, so Steve could work close to home. Christi felt she'd reached her ceiling at World Gym, and it was time to do something new.

We'd heard negatives about working with your spouse: that you spend too much time together, that your relationship can start feeling less like a marriage and more like a business arrangement, that you can lose your entire nest egg, and on and on. These negatives *did* make us wonder if it was a good idea. But we felt we had the right combination of skills, as well as a solid partnership, and those traits would carry us through the experience.

One thing we knew for sure: we wanted to meld our individual skills and talents into something we saw as a workable business, but also something that would fulfill both our passions.

For both of us, it was a conscious decision for Steve to leave his well-paying job so we could start a business. It's a big risk to leave a lucrative position and go in a different direction. With such a big step, you must have the wherewithal to make that decision. You have to put your fears aside and be willing to step out of your comfort zone.

We're not saying that's easy! But it's imperative.

ELEVATE THE ORDINARY

- Consider your personal history. What strengths do your upbringing, education, and relationships bring to the table? How can you use those strengths to take your livelihood to the next level?

- Are there challenges you've faced that actually turned into positives? Can you look at hard times in your life as moments that steered you in a better direction? How can you capitalize on those as you consider starting a business?

- Are you able to remain positive, even when others around you are acting negatively? If you want to manage people and a business, remember that as a business owner, you'll need to always speak positively about people—especially when they're not present.

- If you're considering working with your spouse, begin by taking the pulse of your relationship. Make sure to have open and honest conversations about the pros and cons of working together.

Chapter Two

Can We Really Do This?
Putting the Pieces in Place

WHAT TYPE OF BUSINESS SHOULD WE CREATE?

From the start, our business philosophy was this:

Do what you know, what you enjoy—AND what serves a greater good.

For us, this was a pretty simple equation. We had a mutual interest in sports, fitness, and staying healthy. Christi had experience in that industry. Steve had experience managing a startup. Opening a fitness center—one that filled a niche in our community—gave us a way to merge our talents and passions, both individually and as a couple.

PASSION, PURPOSE, AND SKILLS

The common saying is, do something you love. That may sound trite, but there's truth to it, especially if you want to be an entrepreneur. But you need to think about what you love *and* what you do well. Then, you need to think about how you can turn that into a viable business idea.

We were fortunate to realize early on that entrepreneurship requires three key elements: passion, purpose, and skills.

Passion: We've always said, even during hard times, we want to love our work. We want to be able to ask each other, "Is there something else we'd rather be doing?" and respond firmly, "No—there is nothing we'd rather do than this."

Purpose: The above being said, it's important to remember that passion, in and of itself, is probably more responsible for more small businesses folding than anything else.

Steve says, "Just because I'm passionate about tennis, that doesn't mean I can make a living playing the game. If I tried to do that, it would not be a smart business move for me. I have to be honest with myself: I don't have the talent or drive to play tennis as a career. It's great to have passion for something, whether it's a hobby or work. But for starting a business, purpose should be the goal."

What does that mean? It means that your business needs to fulfill a purpose not just for yourself, but also for your community. If you can marry those two things, a purpose for others and a purpose for yourself, your chances of persevering when the rough times hit are much higher.

Skills: The third piece of the puzzle is to examine your skill set. It's very difficult to build a skill set *and* start a business at the same time. If there's an area you're interested in, but you have little experience in that area, it's a good idea to become trained in that field and work in the field first to gain expertise, before going out on your own.

A LEAP OF FAITH

When we began talking about starting a business, an important question we asked each other was, "What's the worst that can happen?"

We're fortunate to both be positive, optimistic people. We recognized that our positivity is a strength. It's a quality that attracted us to each other when we first met.

When we asked ourselves, "What's our worst-case scenario?" the answer was bankruptcy. But we were young, with one small child. We knew that if our fitness center didn't work out, we had our college degrees, and we believed in our skill sets. Even if we had to crawl back from bankruptcy, we felt confident that we'd be able to do it.

Steve says, "I remember thinking, well, if God closes the door on this, He's got something better for us. That may sound idealistic, but that's just how I'm wired."

Anytime you take a leap of faith toward a new venture, there's a lot of excitement and energy. But there's also fear. It's completely natural to fear the unknown. Unfortunately, many people don't take risks, even calculated risks, because they fear failure.

It *is* scary to venture out on your own in the business world. But if you do it, you'll never have to say, "I wonder what would have happened if I'd tried that?"

TRADEOFFS

We find inspiration in leadership books written by John C. Maxwell. One thing Maxwell talks about is that there are tradeoffs no matter what job you take or what business you start. It's important to understand your particular tradeoffs *before* you take the job, *before* you start the business. It's smart to identify those ahead of time, because that will help you better navigate when it happens.

A lot of people jump into starting a business and say, "Well, I have no idea how I'll make this work. I guess I'll figure it out as I go." They don't intentionally map it out, and that can lead to extreme stress and anxiety later on.

THE PLAN

From the start, we understood that beyond having an initial concept, our plan for the business required several key elements: adequate finances, a suitable location, and a sound, written business plan.

How Much Money Do We Really Need? We knew we'd need start-up capital and a loan to launch our business concept. Our cars were paid off, so we decided to sell them and finance less expensive cars instead. This was the first sign we were serious about our endeavor. Saying goodbye to the BMW 325i and the Mazda Miata wasn't easy. We took pictures, then sold them. We scraped together $50,000 of savings, then started looking at properties to rent and considered our buildout costs.

We soon realized we'd need another $50,000 to get started. In order to secure a loan, our bank told us we'd need to submit a full business plan. We had a general concept of what we wanted to do, but we didn't know anything about writing a business plan. Time for Steve to use everything he'd learned in business school! He went to the library to look at sample business plans before carefully crafting ours.

One business plan (and personal guarantee) later, the loan officer approved our first business loan. We were able to get an unsecured loan for $50,000. That gave us $100,000 of start-up money.

It's important to note that this was in 1997, with the plan of opening a small fitness center in Vero Beach, Florida. Our financial figures should not be used as a basis of comparison for starting your own business. Every business idea is different, with numerous variables. Make sure to carefully consider your own variables as you create your business plan.

Location. As we shopped around, we soon learned that the best locations come with a price. Indian River County is made up of about 160,000 people. It includes a mainland area and a barrier island with the Indian River separating them. The heart of the residential area on the mainland was our target. We narrowed it down to a 4,200-square foot space at a strip plaza on a main road parallel to the busiest highway through Vero Beach. The rent was $6.00 per square foot, compared to $12.00 per square foot to be one block west of the primary route through town.

The owner of a building a mile away from our chosen location strongly advised against it. He suggested (not surprisingly) that *his* location was far superior—for a higher rent, of course. He told us, "You'll never get anyone from the beach side to go there." By "beach side," he meant the barrier island, which is the most affluent area of Vero Beach. It was a ten-minute drive to our chosen location. That owner's location was only a little closer. Steve's honest reaction? The guy's words felt arrogant and self-serving. And it made Steve want to prove him wrong.

However, the location we decided on was in the heart of the competition. There were five fitness facilities operating within a two-mile radius of us. Even Steve's parents thought we were a "little ambitious" to enter into this very competitive industry.

But the reality is, you *need* a competitive spirit to be an entrepreneur. Steve played competitive tennis in high school, college, and afterwards. Steve says, "Competition is in my DNA. And it *really* rises up if someone tells me I can't do something."

These challenges lit Steve's competitive fire. Could we capture that "beach side" demographic *and* enjoy the lower operating costs of a reasonably priced location?

Our Plan. Steve drew up a floor plan for a front desk, two studios, and a babysitting room. Our concept was to have moms doing group exercise while their children were in a gymnastics class. This was in contrast to just offering babysitting, which is what most clubs did. It wasn't flashy, but it was a niche Christi lived and believed in.

OUR NICHE: ADULT GROUP EXERCISE AND KIDS' GYMNASTICS

With Christi's extensive experience in gymnastics, we introduced that into the business. We wanted to take her experience and turn it into an opportunity for kids to learn about activity, exercise, and even structured skills, but the idea wasn't based on it solely being a moneymaker. It was that Christi had seen what gymnastics did for her in *her* life, and she wanted to apply that to our business.

Christi says, "Gymnastics' blend of conditioning, agility, and motor skills is great for very young kids. At a young age, it's such a natural fit. For two-to-four-year-olds, the skills they learn in gymnastics serve them in any other activity they do, then and in ensuing years. For parents, they have the knowledge that their kids are involved in something active while the parent is working out. It became a niche that separated us from the other clubs."

This business model worked because of the three key elements we talked about earlier: *passion, purpose, and skills.*

When it came to both gymnastics and adult fitness classes, Christi had passion and skills. And our model—one-stop shopping for adult fitness and kids' gymnastics—fulfilled a purpose in our community. There were other gymnastics businesses in our community that opened and then subsequently closed within a few years, because they didn't have that winning combination of passion, purpose, and skills.

Our space was 4,200 square feet, with studios for fitness classes and kids' gymnastics. We also had a babysitting room for the littlest ones and the kids who didn't want to be in gymnastics. But we encouraged families to enroll their kids in our structured gymnastics programs, and many of them did.

WHAT'S IN A NAME?

In Vero Beach by this time, Christi was well known in the fitness industry. World Gym, where Christi had worked for years, was huge in Vero Beach when they started, because it was the first fitness franchise in the community. At that time (1993), one of the big clubs had just closed their doors, so much of the fitness business in the community moved to World Gym. Christi was teaching numerous classes there, and she had strong connections in the community. This was a large part of our reasoning for using her name in our business name.

We were fortunate that her parents named her as they did. "Christi's Fitness" has a better ring to it than "Steve's Fitness" ever could!

At the same time, we *did* worry that the name might be a deterrent when it came time to sell. We always knew we'd sell someday, and we were trying to think long term. We were concerned a buyer wouldn't be attracted by that name. We weren't World Gym, after all, or 24-Hour Fitness, or any of the other nationally recognized names.

But our worries turned out to be unfounded, for two reasons. For one thing, in a small community like Vero Beach, when someone has name recognition and a personal connection, the business feels more trustworthy. The power of naming our business Christi's Fitness, and Christi being not only the owner but also an exercise physiologist, someone well educated and trained in the industry, gave the business credibility.

Secondly, the entity who buys a business can change the name, if they prefer. If you're in an urban, highly populated area, a personal name may not be as powerful as it is in a small, rural community where people get to know you. But that's okay; the name can always be changed when and if the business changes hands.

We started out calling our business Christi's Fitness and Weight Management. When we opened our doors, we had a very structured weight management program, along with group exercise and the children's gymnastics program. But over time, we learned that most people weren't comfortable going to a fitness facility for weight loss counsel. Stand-alone weight loss centers do much better than weight loss programs at a health club.

We think the perception people have is that when they walk into a health club, they should already be fit. We've talked to people who say, "I just need to lose about ten or fifteen pounds and then I'll join the gym. I can't do it until then, because everyone will be looking at me."

Of course, nothing could be further from the truth. The reality is, our club and most other fitness centers have members of all body shapes. But the perception that health clubs are for people who are already in shape is out there. It's simply a reality of the industry.

BUILDOUT, DONE RIGHT

We were getting close to opening, and money was tight. So, Steve took on some painting and minor construction duties. He spent long days and late nights painting the interior walls. He picked out a nice beige color, to go with most everything.

Steve says, "What a relief when I finished that paint job. I've always loved looking back at what I've accomplished, when a project is done. Even mowing the lawn is fulfilling for me."

But then he goes on: "As I drove up to the club the next day, looking forward to enjoying the finished paint job, I looked through the window and I saw a pink hue on the walls. *What*? Must be the window tint or the angle. As I entered the building, I couldn't believe the color. It looked pink! *No*! How is this possible? As I discovered after looking at the chip on the color palette from which I chose my 'beige,' it was toward the 'red' end of the spectrum. Argh! Now what? There was no question—I'd have to pick a better beige and then repaint everything."

Steve's "have to do it right" philosophy, going all the way back to his high school job at the convenience store, is hardwired into his brain. There was no way he could live with those pink walls.

In all honesty, though, we did have a beautiful space. Inside, it was modest, but well designed and well appointed. Steve's work in agriculture had connected him with a plant nursery owner in Apopka, Florida. A generous man, the nursey owner offered to fill our new gym with beautiful plants for the grand opening, at no charge. He told us that a business should always use real, living plants. He explained that it shows the business is in it for the long run.

The plants were one more thing to maintain, but if we nurtured them, they stayed healthy and beautiful. It was a metaphor for how we wanted our business to grow. The plants required light, water, and a little plant food. In return, they thrived and beautified our space.

It's the same with people. If you nurture them with kindness and generosity, it allows them to grow and flourish. We wanted to have that sort of relationship with our community.

GAME ON! PRESALES AND GRAND OPENING

While we were building out our space, Steve attended a conference on how to do an effective presale for a health club opening. According to what he learned, we were behind schedule. A four-month presale period was recommended, and we were two months away from our scheduled opening.

The buildout was going well, but we had no experience attracting potential members or selling memberships. We did have the advantage of an anticipated January first opening, good timing for the health club industry.

We set up a presale desk, hoping to sign up as many members as possible. Traffic was light, and we were concerned about the presale numbers. Then one day, a green Ford Explorer drove up.

Steve says, "I'll never forget it. It was the manager of the largest health club in our area, located a mile away. Here I was, face to face with 'The Competition.' He asked us why we were going through all of this; it was like he was certain we'd fail. He said 'Why don't you both just come work for me? What do you want to be paid? $35,000, $40,000?' I guess I should have taken it as a compliment, but instead it just stoked my internal competitive fire. It couldn't have been more motivating. *Game on*."

Presales were lower than we'd hoped for, but when we opened the doors, we had fifty members—enough to get Christi's Fitness and Weight Management into the game.

We were official business owners. We were on our way.

ELEVATE THE ORDINARY

- Horticulturist tip: If you use live plants in your facility, they show you are in it for the long run.
- Does your idea make sense business-wise? Is it marketable? Is there a need for it in your community? Consider how you'll get a piece of the market. What are you going to do differently than other business owners, to break into your market?
- Consider questions like, "How am I going to raise my family at the same time as I run this business?" "How will I create downtime for myself?" "What happens if my business fails?"

- If you've never written a business plan, research and learn how to do so. Use realistic figures for your area, your type of business, and the size of your proposed business. Make sure you have your plan in place before approaching lending institutions.
- What is your niche? What need does your business fulfill in your community that no other business does?
- When naming your business, think about your community, name recognition, and which elements of your chosen name could potentially attract—or deter—future customers. People should be able to know what you do from your name. Remember, too, that many businesses change names over time. Start out with the best name you can come up with, but be prepared to be flexible, in order to meet market demands.

Chapter Three

Startup: Early Years in the Business

DIFFERENT STRENGTHS

From the start, we realized that as business partners as well as husband and wife, having distinctive strengths gave us balance in running a company together. We separated out into our strengths, which greatly benefited both the business and our relationship.

For example, Christi has strong organizational skills. Over time, our scope of services became so broad that if Christi hadn't had those skills, the business wouldn't have done as well as it did.

Moreover, each of us found that it was powerful to be able to discuss our specific areas with someone who had a very different perspective, and then combine that person's input with our own as we made a decision. We would often have long discussions about a decision that had to be made in Steve's area or Christi's area, but in the long run, if it was Christi's area, she made the final decision, and vice versa.

Steve says, "Having a different perspective, especially from a woman and someone who thinks differently, was a great lesson for me. It helped me realize that sometimes my pride could get in the way."

Another thing we learned: the more well-defined responsibilities are, the better, not only between the two of us, but also as the business grew and we began to delegate to employees.

HANGING ON

After we'd been in business for a while, a number of our staff members told us a version of this story:

"I'd drive by," the employee would say. "This was before I worked for you guys. And I'd look at your little place and think, *they'll be out of business in a year.*"

This was a logical assumption on their part. Especially in a small community like Vero Beach, people see so many fitness enterprises come and go. Why should ours be any different?

Looking back, perhaps it was by sheer determination and perseverance that we stayed in business. We didn't have much time or marketing dollars for generating presales. The concept was fulfilling a need for parents who wanted a place to work out while their kids took gymnastics classes. Our target market was moms in their twenties or thirties with small children.

It was slow going in the beginning, but early on, that wasn't such a bad thing. We started small, but back then we could get to know everyone and it felt like a family.

FLEXING OUR SPACE

Our gymnastics space was an open room with carpet and a foam-loaded floor. We also had a studio with a wood floor for aerobics classes. We had a babysitting room and a front desk. That was pretty much it.

We quickly found that if we wanted to attract more members, we needed to add to our adult offerings. We bought some spin bikes and put them in the gymnastics room. We offered spin classes during times when we didn't have kids' gymnastics classes. When it was time for the kids' classes, we'd roll the spin bikes away and pull out gymnastics mats and bars.

KIDS' PROGRAMS: RETHINKING OUR MODEL

As with many fitness centers, our adult programs ran on a membership model. You paid for a membership and committed for a certain period of time, usually six months or a year. You could take unlimited classes while your membership was valid.

Early on, we began using electronic funds transfer for billing, instead of sending invoices. This was in the late 1990s, when this wasn't as typical as it is today. Back then, it took a level of trust for people to give you their credit card or checking account information. But it turned out to be a very important administrative step in our business life.

At first, we ran our kids' gymnastics program the way most gymnastics centers do: using a model of children attending an eight- to ten-week session. At the end of the session, there'd be a week break, and then parents would sign up their kid and pay for the next session.

We realized it would be advantageous to administer our gymnastics program similar to our adult membership. So we put every children's program on a month-to-month programming schedule. The programs never had a beginning or an end. Unless parents cancelled their kids' classes, they just kept taking those classes month to month.

This had a number of advantages:

- It increased and steadied our cash flow.
- It eliminated the gap between sessions, when parents might switch their children to another activity.
- It greatly reduced the time spent on administrative tasks, such as signing up kids and billing parents.
- Children received the benefit of more consistent instruction and quicker improvement.

We offered preschool and recreational classes at different levels. Teachers continually evaluated kids for skill sets. A student could be in a level for three months, they could be there for eight months, they could be there for a year and a half. It depended on the motivation of the child and their consistency attending classes.

Steve says, "Teaching preschool gymnastics isn't easy. Ask Christi. She would come out of the gymnastics room after chasing three- and four-year-olds for forty-five minutes, and her hair was in knots. It looked like she'd been wrestling with them."

Although it sometimes seemed like they weren't learning anything, those kids *were* listening. And they did catch on—eventually. Over the years, many of our former preschoolers went on to become competitive gymnasts or excel in another sport. Gymnastics builds upper body, lower body, and core strength, as well as flexibility. It also teaches children to set goals and discipline themselves to achieve them. These skills are a great foundation for any future athletics, and they teach valuable life lessons at the same time.

Staffing was another challenge we faced with our gymnastics program. Finding people who loved working with children wasn't easy. We pursued mothers and schoolteachers; both of these groups made great beginner gymnastics coaches. But working late afternoons and early evenings, part time, was inconvenient for them. They were a great asset once we had them trained, but getting them to stick around was difficult. There's a high level of burnout.

Every community has a need for preschool programs, but in Vero Beach, as in most places, it's difficult recruiting people to teach those classes. It takes patience to find and develop coaches who have a passion for teaching such young kids. It was a constant process to find people who were aligned with our goals and values, but that's what set our children's programs apart.

Another obstacle with our kids' programs was parents trusting us to teach their children. Successful, long-lasting preschool programs have great leaders, people who lead by example and show they believe in the program's benefits for children. That's rare, and that was us—but since we were new at the game, it took a while before we had a reputation in the community that enticed large numbers of parents to sign up their children for our programs.

Over time, we added more options for kids: dance classes, Mommy and Me, martial arts, and Speed Academy (agility and speed training). In our new facility (which we'll talk about in Chapter Eight), we had a pool, so we added swimming. By the time we sold the business in 2018, we had so many children's programs, there were about 750 kids coming through the facility during any given week.

"If it doesn't scare you, you're probably not dreaming big enough." – Tory Burch

---

HOW MUCH DO WE WANT THIS?

Our early days in business were exciting, but scary. But that's part of stepping out in faith, there are no guarantees.

Fortunately, filling and staffing the adult group exercise classes in the early years wasn't as much of a concern as with the kids' classes. Christi was known in our area for quality adult group exercise instruction.

That being said, Steve remembers coming up to the traffic light just south of the plaza that housed our fitness center and immediately scrutinizing the parking lot, praying there would be at least five cars. Christi said we needed at least five or six people in a class to make it work. Thank heaven, we usually had that many!

To "expand his portfolio" (businessman's term for "save money on payroll expenses") Steve became certified to teach spin classes. We were the first health club to bring this new style of group exercise class to the community. Those classes were filling up, and members were excited.

Steve says, "I enjoyed teaching, but at times, it was a real gut check. I'd be heading to the club with my four-year-old son screaming in the back seat because he didn't want to go. In my head, I'm tallying how much money we're losing, and at the same time trying to sort out my music for my cycling class that would start in ten minutes. But when I reached Christi's, I had to get myself in the game. I'd head inside, fake a smile that I hoped made it look like we were making money, try to peel my crying son from my leg to drop him off in the babysitting room, and then slap a big grin on my face, ready to teach cycling. Many times, I remember thinking, *I'm not sure I can do this.* But forty-five minutes later, after some sweat, endorphins, and a few compliments from members, I'd survived another day."

As a business owner, it's times like these that you might ask yourself, *how much do I want this? How much do I want to succeed?* You have to keep answering that question by saying, *enough to keep going, no matter what it takes or how hard it is.* If you want to be in business for yourself, perseverance is a must.

There were six gyms within three miles of ours. We worried about the competition. But we tried to remain optimistic.

Steve says, "Christi always had a great attitude, and it helped me keep one too, especially during the lean years. It amazed me how she was able to find the upside in a down situation. One memorable day, I delivered the somber news that after paying the bills, there was no money left. I'll never forget her response: 'Well, it's good we had enough to pay the bills.' That kind of attitude is a lifeboat (or at least a bilge pump) when the ship is taking on water."

TAKING A CHANCE IN ORDER TO GROW

Our first years were lean. All right—they were anorexic. We were undercapitalized. There was some traction with membership, but it was very slow. After two years, we had 175 members and were still operating in the red.

When you start a business, you have high hopes that it will be an instant success. For most entrepreneurs (including us), nothing anyone says can dissuade you from that notion! But your checkbook will.

Because of this, you do every necessary task. You do whatever it takes. This isn't a bad thing, because you not only develop a great work ethic, but it helps later on when you need to lead other people doing those tasks.

Even so, we weren't gaining the momentum we needed. We said to each other, "If we keep going on this path, it looks like we're heading more and more into the red. Why don't we take a chance on creating a bigger market by adding some treadmills and a weight room?"

Steve went to our landlord and asked him, "If we rent another thousand square feet, can you lower the rent rate, not only for the new space but also for our existing space?"

The landlord could see that we were trying to do right by the community. Probably just as importantly, his daughters were coming to our facility with their children. Our landlord's little granddaughter was taking gymnastics classes from us. So he agreed. When we'd first opened, our rent was around seven dollars a square foot. Each time we expanded, he'd drop it a little more. Eventually, we were paying slightly under six dollars a square foot.

But we were also helping him. Ultimately, we took up six of the nine bays in the building, and our space represented 13,000 square feet of his 21,000-square foot facility.

But when he agreed to our first expansion at a lower rent, the landlord didn't know how well it would work out. At that time, he was willing to help because he saw the good in what we were trying to do. When you're genuine about what you do, you can always find people who will pull for you.

FUNDING OUR EXPANSION

Of course, not everyone was on our side, the way the landlord was. Besides more space, we also needed additional capital in order to expand. We went back to the bank to ask for more money. But they wanted us to pay back our existing loan before they'd give us another loan.

What could we do? We didn't want to bring in a partner that we'd have to answer to. We'd consciously decided we wanted autonomy. We were a sole proprietorship for the first few years, and then a Chapter S Corporation the rest of the time we owned the business.

But the reality was, there wasn't enough money coming in to pay the bills, much less to expand and set up a weight and cardio machine room. Enter the credit cards. The cards helped pay for capital improvements on our existing facility.

By the time we'd expanded twice, we had $200,000 worth of credit card debt. What we'd hoped for came to fruition: the new offerings brought in additional members. So, our membership grew, but we'd also taken on more rent, more overhead, and more staff. The membership hadn't built up sufficiently to cover all those new costs.

We can admit it now: taking on that much credit card debt was incredibly risky. We don't recommend this strategy, of course. In retrospect, we were undercapitalized, and we underestimated how long it would take to generate positive cash flow.

THERE WILL ALWAYS BE NAYSAYERS

One thing we realized is that no matter what you do, someone is sure to let you know why they think it won't work.

Our expanded space was in the back half of a bay that housed a discount grocery store. Steve says, "I remember one day a guy dropping off grocery supplies told me we'd never make it, because fitness is such a vain business. I tried to explain to him about the kids in gymnastics and how the moms weren't yelling at their kids as much, but he wasn't having it. Some people will just try to discourage you."

Less than a year later, the grocery store was gone and we took the front half of that bay, as well as another full bay adjacent to the other side of the facility.

At that time, Steve sketched out a drawing to reconfigure the entire space, which was now 8,000 square feet. We did all the work on the interior ourselves, configuring it to meet our needs. We now had a much wider range of offerings for the community.

What we learned from that experience is this: business is like gambling, except you have the ability to stack the deck. But it's imperative to know when to listen and who to listen to. In our case, that was our members, who were asking for amenities we weren't offering at first.

BUYING SMART

If you've ever gone shopping with money to burn, you know that sometimes it's more of a curse than a blessing, because you simply can't decide what to get.

Making buying decisions when you don't have much money is different. You naturally seek out the lowest price. But if you don't exercise smart decision-making when you shop on a tight budget, especially as a business owner, it can cost you later.

From the start, we decided that listening to our members was the backbone of our business, even if they were asking for expensive equipment. This was easier said than done. When we shopped around for cardio equipment, the sticker shock was real. A new treadmill or elliptical ran upwards of $4,000. What to do? After researching options, we found a company that sold reconditioned cardio equipment at half the cost of new.

We also located a start-up equipment vendor. It was owned by a former employee of one of the big-brand strength machine companies, so they knew what they were doing. Their equipment was half the price of the big-brand guys. We were on our way to outfitting our first weight room.

Having fewer resources forces you to buy smart. It encourages digging in and doing your homework.

There's another benefit: buying smart involves developing deeper relationships with people. We came to truly appreciate these vendors we worked with. As with our landlord, they were a blessing, at a time when we needed it most.

ADDITIONAL REVENUE STREAM: SUMMER CAMPS

In year four, after we'd expanded our space, we began running summer camps. Our camps were a full day, and we ran the program for five to seven weeks. In addition to gymnastics, there were various other elements added to the camps as we grew, such as dance, crafts, swimming and roller skating excursions.

The summer camps were a great way to generate revenue during the summer, which tends to be slow in our seasonal community, particularly for children's programs. Many kids participated in our year-round program, but in the summer, some parents pulled kids out because they were traveling or doing other activities.

Offering camps gave us the ability to generate income, even if kids were only coming for a week or two.

We had between five and ten counselors each summer, most of them college students. This was in Christi's area, and she always honored the counselors at the end of the summer with a celebration. She'd take them to a Japanese steakhouse or the Melting Pot, something kind of high-end for most of them, at their age. One year, Christi took them to Universal Studios.

A key element of our counselor appreciation program was that Christi always went along for the end-of-summer event. She didn't send another staff member to "represent management." Christi wanted the counselors to know that appreciation for them came from the top.

BEING OPEN TO CHANGE

Everyone will tell you how important it is to be willing to change and adapt. That's never truer than it is when running your own business.

We learned to avoid using the words, "This is the way we've always done it." Instead we'd consider the question, "Do we keep it this way because it's a great system, or do we re-evaluate and possibly make a change for the better?"

Tweaking Our Model for Kids' Classes. An example of this is parents who cancelled their child's participation in gymnastics classes. When we began asking parents why they were cancelling, we found that often the reason was because the child had been in the same level too long. Why was that? When we took the time to truly think about it, we wondered if it might be related to class frequency. They were only coming one time per week, and normal absences slowed down their progression.

Steve asked, "Instead of kids coming once a week for a flat fee of $50 a month, what if we had them come twice a week for $80 a month? It would mean teaching double the classes, but if the kids have more repetition, won't they progress to the next level faster?"

Christi agreed that they would. "One class a week is the norm in the industry," she said. "It's what you find in most places, unless parents sign up their kid for twice a week. But it's true that frequency vastly improves their skills. Another benefit is that coaches would get to know their students better if they saw them twice a week."

When we implemented this change, we received positive feedback all around. Parents wanted to see their kids achieving goals. And the kids were thrilled with how their skills developed.

Around this time, we also added in-house competitions for gymnastics students. We knew that other sports programs for kids had ribbons and trophies at the end of the season or the year. To help with our students' sense of accomplishment, we did the same.

Everyone wants to feel successful, even kids. (Maybe especially kids!) And as every parent knows, a child who feels successful will continue to be motivated.

Expanded Hours. At first, we were closed in the middle of the day. We opened early in the morning for spin and adult fitness classes, with a few preschool gymnastics classes. We closed midday, then opened later in the afternoon for more gymnastics, fitness classes, and spin.

But in the perception of most people, a health club is somewhere you go when you want to. Particularly when we expanded our services, offering a weight room and cardio equipment, limited hours wouldn't work. People wanted to be able to come in and use the equipment at a time that fit their schedules. So, in year three, when we added the weight room and cardio machines, we began opening during the middle of the day. Our hours became 5:30 a.m. to 9:00 p.m., Monday through Saturday.

Initial Name Change. When we renamed the business from Christi's Fitness and Weight Management to Christi's Family Fitness, Steve's father said, "I don't like that. I'm worried you're limiting your market."

Steve replied, "Dad, who *isn't* part of a family?"

But we knew what he meant. With a name like Christi's Family Fitness, our facility would be perceived as more kid-oriented than adult-oriented.

We made a conscious business decision to be at peace with that. Since we were running so many successful kids' programs as our niche, we decided the name change worked for us. Adults without kids would either use the facility, or they wouldn't. Our market would now be six-month-olds to ninety-year-olds.

Key to this decision is that we were open to changing the name again if we had to. We always remained open to change and new ways of doing things.

RETURN ON *REINVESTMENT*

It's desirable to see an attractive return on our investments. That goes for retirement plans, real estate, and other major life choices. But what does it mean to have a return on a *re*investment?

To us, it means not just spending money on the right things, but also continually reinvesting in relationships and people. If you're only looking at your profit margin, you miss out on one of the greatest blessings of running a business: doing it for others.

Anyone can repair a broken water fountain, fix equipment, or clean the floor. But *when* do you replace the fountain, buy new equipment, put down new flooring, or repaint? The best answer is, before your customers tell you it needs to be done.

Word of mouth is your best marketing tool—better than any advertising dollar you'll ever spend. But if customers continually have to remind you to take care of the basics, you might not be building a brand they deem worthy of recommending to friends and family.

In addition to covering your basics, it's important to continually up your game. Adding amenities gives customers confidence in your company, which translates into retention and loyalty. Additions don't always have to be expensive. Sometimes the smallest things mean the most. For us, that meant things like hairdryers and containers of Q-tips in the locker rooms, and additional seating throughout our facility. These little things showed that we were listening and we cared about our members.

Fresh new offerings are also vital. Paying attention to trends demonstrates a passion for your industry and sets your business apart from the competition.

For example, when small group training became popular, we rented space across the street, relocated a dance program, and renovated our old dance studio into a small group training playground. We researched and bought into a franchised program, bringing our members the latest in coach-led, interval-based, small group training.

We also created a second, upscale industrial-modern 3,000-square foot facility housing a boutique-style studio. In addition to dance, this allowed us to use that space for mind-body classes, which were becoming popular at the time. We also had a private Pilates room for one-on-one sessions and a separate acupuncture room. There were small, boutique-style facilities popping up in our area, running similar programs, but because we offered these classes in addition to our other programming, members stayed with us instead of defecting to other facilities. It spoke loudly to both our members and our staff that we expanded again and stayed current in fitness industry offerings.

As discussed above, for many years, we bought used equipment out of necessity. Once our budget allowed us to buy new, we did. Again, it made a statement to staff and members that we had up-to-date technology throughout both clubs.

FIGHTING A BAD RAP

While gyms have helped many people become healthier, the fitness industry still fights a negative reputation. So many clubs close their doors overnight, often declaring bankruptcy and leaving members high and dry. This makes it difficult for fitness facilities to be viewed as viable, stable businesses. When we started in 1997, both banks and potential members looked at the fitness industry as risky business.

The sales practices many clubs employ create another downside of the industry. Pressuring people to join before they're ready contributes to buyer remorse and a negative perception of the industry as a whole.

Before we opened our facility, we made a conscious decision not to apply pressure tactics in presales. That might have been one of the reasons our presales numbers were lower than we'd have liked. But because we didn't use pressure tactics, the majority of our presale customers stuck around.

We've always been big believers in the Golden Rule. The quote in the English Standard Version of The Bible is, "So whatever you wish that others would do to you, do also to them." (Matthew 7:12)

While we find these particular words inspiring, the advice to "do unto others as you would have them do unto you" applies regardless of an individual's belief system. Running our business, we decided we'd simply treat people the way we wanted to be treated.

We did things our industry would consider "radical." We responded to price inquiries over the phone, without insisting people come into the gym for an "appointment." We posted our pricing online and didn't veer from it. We didn't pressure people or play games with them to persuade them to join our club.

When you constantly run specials, people who paid full price don't appreciate it. We knew we'd retain more members with consistent pricing than we would by jumping from one "special deal" to the next.

Our feeling has always been that if a person is treated like a friend, not like a wallet, God honors that. This goes back to the Golden Rule. When we're on the customer side of a business transaction, we want to be treated as if that business's owner truly cares about us. So why wouldn't we want the same for our own customers?

Advertising and promoting our programs and amenities was great, but ultimately, it was about filling the club with people who decided on their own that our gym was a good fit for them. Our retention on paid-in-full memberships was consistently above 75%, which was 15% to 20% higher than the national average.

The fitness industry is constantly trying to solve dual problems: members cancelling before their membership expires, and getting previous members to come back. We solved both of these problems in a straightforward way: by applying our lifelong values to our business model.

Sounds simple? That's because it is. And it works.

APPRECIATE EVERYONE

Remember our landlord, whom we talked about earlier? Here's one more story about him, one that reiterates our feelings about the Golden Rule.

The term "landlord" implies power. As a renter, you're being "lorded" over. Dealing with the building owner you rent from might feel intimidating. But if you apply the same respect and care to this relationship as you take with your customers, it can be a rewarding experience.

In year four of owning our club, after it looked like we'd be able to sustain the business, one day Steve called the landlord, simply to thank him for helping make our dream a reality.

There was no response. Steve thought the line had gone dead.

But it hadn't. The landlord was just gathering his thoughts. Finally, he said, "I have never before received a call from a tenant that wasn't about a problem or some kind of request."

Our landlord appreciated being recognized and sincerely thanked. Every person appreciates this. And it's something that happens far too infrequently in our society.

But that man truly helped us. He was in business, too. He had to take risks, secure a mortgage, pay property taxes and insurance, and hope someone would rent his space. He deserved our thanks.

Over the years, we expanded three more times. Each time, the landlord invited Steve out to his farm and talked about his horses, his children, and his grandchildren. He became not just our landlord, but also our friend.

Steve says, "We had eight years in his building and many great memories. But my favorite is that phone call. *Everyone* needs to feel appreciated and valued. Even landlords."

ELEVATE THE ORDINARY

- If you have a partner, how can you separate business duties to utilize each of your strengths? In what ways can you support each other in your distinct areas?
- If you need to invest in equipment or materials, what techniques can you use to "buy smart"? In what ways can you be creative in your purchases, making money stretch further without sacrificing quality?
- Do you find yourself saying, "This is the way we've always done it"? If so, think about innovative ideas you might use to improve results.
- Do you truly appreciate your customers? Do they show it, in the form of return business and referrals? If not, in what ways could you modify your business practices to apply the Golden Rule to your customer relationships? What about your other business relationships?

CHAPTER FOUR

BUILDING A CULTURE, PART ONE: EMPLOYEES

MISSION STATEMENT, VISION STATEMENT, AND CORE VALUES

A company's *mission statement* defines the purpose of the company. In contrast, a *vision statement* is focused on future objectives. *Core values* are a group's beliefs, stated at a very basic level.

Why should you develop these pieces for your business? One reason is that when you're struggling with a decision (and guaranteed, sometimes you *will* struggle with decisions), you can go back to your mission statement, vision statement, and core values to ask yourself, "When we make this decision, which choice aligns with what defines our company?"

We developed a mission statement, vision statement, and core values when we'd been in business for about six years. In retrospect, we wish we'd done it sooner. We added these items to our employee handbook. This helped employees understand who we were and what we stood for.

Five years later, our leadership team got together to revise these pieces. (Yes, by then we had a leadership team, comprised of many more people than just Steve and Christi.) It's a good idea to revisit your mission and vision statements and your core values regularly. Moreover, it's important that key staff members play a part in shaping these pieces. (See Appendix A for specifics of the above.)

OUR PRINCIPLES: A DIFFERENTIATOR

We used certain guiding principles to run our business. We believe these principles differentiated us from the competition. Here a few examples:

- Our business relied on biblical principles for guidance. However, we never discussed someone's faith in an interview, and we didn't require staff to believe what we did in order to be part of our company.
- For the first ten years in business, we didn't open on Sundays.
- We used Christian authors as sources for our leadership meetings.
- We advertised on Christian radio.
- We offered a contemporary Christian music spin class.
- We prayed with our staff at every Christmas party and at lunch events.
- Since its inception, we belonged to the Christian Business Association.

These things set a foundation for us as business owners, helping us be authentic and true to our long-held values.

While we found the Bible to be the best guide for this, we never spoke negatively about any other faith. We didn't evangelize to our staff or try to convert them. We simply set a standard for what we believed was important.

One of our goals was to be the highest quality high-end facility in our county. To do that, we had to stand apart from our competition.

Throughout our business life, we had many employees and members comment that one of the major differences they noticed about our culture was that they felt they could trust us. Was this because of our guiding principles? Maybe—but the point is, however you establish trust with your staff and customers, it's one of the most important keys to a successful business.

A CULTURE OF SERVING

Building on what we said above, a key component of our mission statement, vision statement, and core values was our culture of serving. We worked to hire staff who had a good work ethic and were teachable. We wanted people who were willing to learn and open to serving. We believe that this, too, differentiated us from the competition. A genuine, serving heart is the biggest differentiator any business can have.

We had a sign in the gymnastics room that said something to the effect of, "It's a privilege to work with children." We knew kids looked forward all week to class. We owed them our attention, effort, and best attitude.

We wanted coaches to think of their classes not just as a time to teach a skill, but also a time to have fun. We wanted kids to enjoy being with their instructors and classmates. When that happened, we knew we had a great experience going. Combine that with a clean, bright, comfortable facility that appeals to parents, and you can see why it worked.

HIRE CHARACTER FIRST, NOT SKILLS

When it came to hiring, we learned to look for people with the character traits we wanted, rather than simply looking for people whose resumes stated they had the experience for a particular role.

In our rural community, it was rare to find someone with a lot of experience. That being said, if they had experience and our gut instincts told us their personality was a match with our culture, we'd usually bring them on. Sometimes we did that even when we didn't really need them. If they were a good fit character-wise and they had experience, we'd work them in.

Jim Collins, author of *Good to Great*, uses a "bus" metaphor to illustrate this principle. Collins says, "It is better to first get the right people on the bus, the wrong people off the bus, and the right people in the right seats, and then figure out where to drive."

We also asked our "five-star" employees if they had friends who might want to work for us. We realized that people tend to hang out with others who are similar in personality to them. The fact that they were friends was also a benefit, because it created built-in community within the staff.

One of our employees, Don (whom you'll meet later in this chapter), had a huge impact on relationship-building at our facility. When we met him, we could tell right away that he cared about people; he cared about kids. He's got an enormous heart, and his values aligned with our core values. Here we had someone who was trustworthy, someone with integrity, who also had enthusiasm, was great connecting with people, and had a college education. Our instincts told us that Don could learn to do just about any job in our facility.

When we hired Don, it wasn't because he had specific job experience that we were looking for. We'd learned by then that if it was a choice of experience or character, we were always better off hiring for a person's character, then training for skills. Don is a great example of that.

We also involved other staff in the interview process to get their feedback about the potential new hire. This process would give them some ownership in the process and showed them we cared about their input when adding to our staff and culture.

"Unity does not mean sameness. It means oneness of purpose."
– Priscilla Shirer

STAFF DIVERSITY

At first, we thought we needed people just like us. We figured they'd perform like us, which we assumed would be a good thing.

Our first few employees were similar to us. Later, we realized that diversity was a strength of our organization. Our membership represented many different types of people. The employees serving them needed to reflect that, which is something we began to keep in mind when recruiting employees.

While it's typical to gravitate toward people similar to ourselves, it's important not to judge others based on appearance or perception. So often, we size each other up in a single interaction. Why do we do that? How could we possibly know anything about a person within seconds of meeting them?

Several times, homeless members of our community wanted to train at our facility. Sometimes, we ended up employing them, because we wanted to help them get their lives back on track. Although it didn't always work out in the long run, we didn't regret these hires. It was worthwhile to give it a try.

We gave all our employees room to take on more responsibility, as well as make mistakes and learn from them. We realized that unless we took a chance on people, we wouldn't know how much they could grow.

HIRING YOUNG PEOPLE

Because we had difficulty finding enough adults to teach the kids' programs, a lot of high schoolers worked for us. We just made sure they had supervisors who were older.

High schoolers, we found, had the energy to keep up with our preschool students. At the basic levels, we could train a teenager, as long as they loved being with kids. At those levels, we were mostly teaching coordination and motor skills. If a high schooler had great character and loved being around children, we could train them in these basics. We had a very structured training program to make sure they knew their position had a high value and to keep them accountable to our standards.

We looked for teens who were active themselves, even if gymnastics wasn't their thing. It might have been another sport—again, we could train.

Whether a teen or adult, the key was finding great character and letting employees use their strengths. Once an employee was in a role that matched their gifts, usually they flourished.

ARE THEY WHO WE THINK THEY ARE?

Christi hired for the children's programs and adult group exercise. Steve hired front desk, nursery, and support staff. Later, we had department leaders who were in charge of hiring. If we started a new program, Christi began by hiring a director. Then she worked with that director as they hired initial staff for the program.

We found that some potential employees interviewed great and looked good on a resume, but we'd get them in and discover it wasn't the right fit.

For example, in a business like ours, it's important to be smiley and upbeat. When we're having a bad day, most of us don't like to hear the words, "Oh, come on—just smile!" But the reality is, ours was a customer-service-driven industry. Our employees had to reflect that, even on bad days.

If we liked an employee, but they had a trait that wasn't positive for the business, we talked with them about it. We were direct, even though it can be uncomfortable giving a person direct, specific feedback. What if they go on the defensive? You hope they'll understand you want to help them, that you're giving them a shot.

We would gently but firmly say, "We need you to be a little more smiley" or "We need you to be more proactive greeting people, less demure in your stance."

Sometimes, the employee truly worked at it and improved. Other times, even with attempting corrections, it was just their personality. In that case, they weren't a great fit for our company.

Over time, we became better at recognizing such characteristics during interviews. We trained our managers in this, too. Doing so saved everyone—the potential employee, as well as us—lots of heartache.

Even so, we didn't always get it right. Sometimes, it just took time. Steve's mother used to say, "Time heals all ills." Whether that's true or not, one thing we learned while running our business is that time certainly reveals who a person is.

Time also teaches you that everyone has experiences that shape them. We've had employees arrested for domestic battery, skimming cash, and even stealing toilet paper.

We'd never have suspected these employees. But when we heard their full stories, we weren't angry. In a lot of cases, a series of events led to them making bad decisions. We were sympathetic, but that didn't mean there weren't consequences. If an employee made a truly grave mistake, they were terminated. All of our employees knew this and understood it.

In our experience, you can study employees your whole life and still be surprised how a new hire performs after they start working for you. It's back to school, every day.

ONBOARDING

Once an employee is hired, it's only the tip of the iceberg. There's still plenty to do in order to ensure the relationship succeeds.

Certification. In many gyms, as long as an instructor candidate is certified, they're hired. But certification is rarely an indicator of teaching skills. Most certifications can be done over a weekend. If someone is a good memorizer and regurgitator, they can get certified fairly easily.

But that doesn't mean they have the skills to teach. A certified instructor might know the movements to do in a particular class, but not understand what's going on in the body to make those movements happen. Christi only wanted to hire instructors who had strong, in-depth knowledge of human physiology. For this reason, she required all potential instructors to audition with her.

One time, an instructor candidate who was newly certified made numerous mistakes during his audition. Christi advised him to try other facilities, while at the same time working to gain a better understanding of physiology. "By that point, our members were used to a high level of group exercise instruction," Christi says. "We only hired instructors who met our standards."

That instructor took Christi's advice, and later, when he was ready, he came to work for us. He became one of our most popular teachers.

Evaluations. Every year, Christi evaluated our group exercise instructors. She took everyone's class. Plus, she was still teaching her own classes. Eventually, we had close to forty instructors, and it took her three months to evaluate everybody.

Christi says, "Before I owned my own fitness center, I don't think anyone ever came in to evaluate my class, not in any place I taught before opening my own place. But as an owner, I found these evaluations vital. They gave me a chance to connect with each instructor. After I took their class, I sat down with them to talk. Along with the evaluation, I'd catch up on their lives outside of work, their families, their dreams and goals."

The evaluations were across the board. Someone might have been teaching in our facility for fifteen years, but if Christi heard them say something during their class that was incorrect (for example, if they made an anatomical mistake), she brought it to their attention.

"You can't be afraid to have that conversation," Christi says. "It's too important. I balanced it by highlighting what they did well."

We showed appreciation for our staff throughout the year, but meeting individually for a formal review once a year was important to them, and to us.

Trial period. If we let someone go within their first ninety days of working for us, we weren't required to pay unemployment. Knowing this, we trained directors to recognize red flags within that trial period and immediately address them.

It makes financial sense to let go earlier, rather than later. But there's an emotional component, too. The longer you wait, the more connected you can become to the employee. We wished them well, and we wanted them to succeed—but if they weren't working out, it was better for everyone to let go.

For what reasons did we let someone go during their trial period? Often, it was something like repeatedly calling in sick or getting subs. Instead of coming ten minutes early, they were dashing in one minute before their class's start time. They were unwilling to pitch in and help other staff.

We identified these issues as soon as possible. We put expected improvements in writing, with a date when we would follow up. We had the employee sign it.

While we tried, we found that this type of thing often doesn't improve. Usually, people are on their best behavior at the start. If they're doing these types of things from the get-go, the situation is unlikely to improve. But we *did* give them a chance.

Rolling with the punches. Getting the right people on our team was one of our toughest tasks, especially in our small town, where it was hard to find potential employees. Training new hires was equally stressful. There are so many facets of onboarding a new employee. Every day they were with us, they deepened relationships with staff and members. When they worked out, it was all worth it. When we chose to end their employment during the trial period, it was disappointing, but we moved on.

Even harder was when an employee chose to leave after a month or two. We were saddened when that happened, which wasn't often, but we took a deep breath, rolled up our sleeves, and restarted our search.

The reality is, employees coming and going is part of running a business. We found it helped when we began asking interview questions such as:

- What brought you to Vero Beach?
- What do you like about living in this area?
- Why aren't you working now (if that's the case)?
- Why do you want to work for us?

When you find a winner, an "A" player that sticks around, it's like a tailwind at your back. Everything gets a little easier. You see blessings every day.

Unfortunately, we often found that these "A" players wanted to run—and were perfectly capable of running—their *own* business. When that happened, especially with long-term employees, we gave them our best wishes and encouraged them to succeed.

Why? Because we realized they were taking the same opportunity *we'd* taken to be in business for ourselves. Plus, if you reflect on what you've endured as a business owner, you realize your former employees will be rolling with the same body shots you took. All you can do is wish them well.

EMPLOYEE APPRECIATION

Appreciating staff was important to us. We knew they were the backbone of our business, and as our company grew, our success depended on them.

The little things. One of the most important ways to appreciate staff is to get to know them personally. That doesn't mean you need to be their best friend; in fact, keeping a professional distance is wise. But when you find out about a need in an employee's life that you can help with, it shows you see them as a person, not just an employee.

Our appreciation might come in the form of encouragement or referring them to a pastor or counselor. Or it was buying a part for their car or surprising them with a much-needed paid day off. These things were small to us, but they meant a lot to the employee.

Staff birthdays. Christi recognized each employee's birthday, with a card and a small gift. This made employees feel valued and gave them a sense of belonging.

By the time we'd been in business for a dozen years, Christi was recognizing twelve to eighteen birthdays a month. Eventually, she shifted this responsibility to the directors of various areas. This gave the directors another opportunity to connect with their staff. Christi continued to recognize the directors' birthdays, but they were in charge of their staffs' birthdays, and we let them celebrate in the way they saw fit.

Birthdays are special! We wanted to honor each person as an individual and as part of our business family. Simple things can be the most meaningful.

Going above and beyond. An employee can tell when you're using empty words and, conversely, when you've walked in their shoes. We made it a habit to pick up anything lying around that was out of place, or clean up messes (even when we had accidents in the bathroom). Members frequently mentioned they saw us doing these small things, rather than barking orders at someone else to "take care of it." If Christi or Steve was the first person on the scene, *we* took care of it. We trained that by example.

It worked, too. We weren't the only ones who went above and beyond job description. When an employee did this, we made sure to recognize them. We gave them gift cards to Starbucks, Einstein's, Chipotle, or a movie theater. Sometimes, we'd give them a gift card for a manicure, pedicure, or massage.

Again, as we began to have more managers, we handed this responsibility into their hands. Christi bought a bunch of ten-dollar gift cards, as well as note cards. She instructed the managers that if they spotted someone going above and beyond, they should compose a handwritten note, slip in a gift card, and give it to that person.

Again, this was a small thing, but it made people feel recognized and appreciated.

Getting creative. We knew our creativity differentiated us from other clubs, so we were innovative in our approach to making employees feel valued. We'd take employees from a particular department out for lunch, kayaking, or waterskiing. Once, we rented a limo and took a department's staff to the mall, where they were given seventy-five dollars each and told they had thirty minutes, and we wanted them to spend the money completely on themselves. Some people truly struggled to buy things for themselves; they wanted to treat other people instead. That gave us great insight to their character. We hadn't set up the outing as a test of character, but it did tell us much about those individuals.

Christmas party. We took a lot of time planning our staff Christmas party. We often had the party at our home. Or we'd rent out an unusual venue, one capable of hosting large gatherings, like a boat or our city's courthouse.

Rather than standing around eating and chatting, we'd have activities designed to help people connect. Once, we set up an elaborate scavenger hunt. Another year, we had staff members submit baby pictures. We projected them on a screen, and people tried to guess who each one was.

Once, we played an elaborate game that ended in us giving everyone a $100 bill. For our teenaged workers, being handed a hundred dollars was thrilling. And what adult doesn't appreciate extra cash during the holidays?

Steve always gave a speech, which included stories from the year. He told staff about things we'd noticed in the growth of business, and talked about how they were such an important part of that.

The Christmas party was about unity and having fun with each other, outside of the gym. We got to dress up. (At work, most of the time everyone was in tights, shorts, and sneakers.) People could bring their spouse or significant other.

The parties cost $3,000 to $6,000. It was an investment, but we budgeted for it, and it was well worth the money.

RECOGNIZING EVERYBODY

We made sure employee recognition wasn't just about coaches and instructors. It included all staff members.

Welcome desk staff. A fun, innovative way to recognize this team was to take them out to eat, and later evaluate the restaurant. We'd talk about what the host, wait staff, and other employees did well. We'd ask our staff, "What appealed? What didn't?" Talking about these issues helped this key component of our staff—the first people to greet members when they walked in the door—understand how vital their area of our business was.

One time, we took the welcome-desk folks on a moonlight river kayaking trip. We kayaked to a little island and had a meal. Another time, we rented a bus and drove to a park in Orlando that had waterskiing and wake boarding. We all did it for several hours, and we videotaped it.

Babysitting (Kids' Kingdom) staff. We knew that if parents were happy with our children's care while in our babysitting room, they'd continue coming to our gym. Babysitting rooms are common in fitness centers, but often, the workers are left off by themselves and not included as part of the team. Many other clubs would pay them minimum wage. We made sure we compensated our babysitting staff well.

Steve worked shifts in our kids' room, which we called "Kids' Kingdom." (More about that in the next chapter.) Working in Kids' Kingdom helped Steve understand how challenging that work is. He says, "When you experience what your staff experiences, you truly value them. Christi taught a lot of children's classes, so she knew what that was like. I helped out in the babysitting room, which taught me what that's like."

It was the babysitting staff that we took to the mall. When they got in the limo, they didn't know where we were going. We gave them money and instructed them to spend it on themselves, then meet us back at the food court, where everyone shared what they'd bought.

As with other employee appreciation adventures, we went along. We knew that if we were there, it meant more to them than just their director taking them.

DEPARTMENTAL STAFF MEETINGS

- As our business grew, we added directors:
- Dance
- Gymnastics
- Swim
- Mommy and Me
- Nursery
- Welcome desk
- Personal training

…as well as others. We asked the directors of these areas to meet several times a year with their teams. The idea was to have an educational component, as well as provide an opportunity to connect.

When a department was in a meeting like this, they were on the clock but not doing their regular jobs. Doing the math, it cost us $300 to $400 to have a departmental meeting. But in the big picture, it was worth it. Everyone feels scattered at times, but when a group periodically comes together like this, they function better as a team.

COMPENSATION

Figuring out compensation is one of the trickiest parts of running a business. It will vary, of course, depending on the nature of your business and your employees. But over the years, we discovered a few universal concepts around employee pay that worked well for us.

Levels of pay. Staff need to be paid, of course, but they all don't need to be paid the same. Even within the same job description, there can be varying levels of pay. Everyone deserves an annual review and, if warranted, a raise. But there are a lot of factors involved in determining a wage that makes sense for both the business owner and the employee.

In his book *Good to Great*, Jim Collins explains how a business is like a large, horizontal disc spinning on an axis. In the beginning, it's hard to just get it moving. The right people help you push the disc to spin it faster the same direction you're pushing. The wrong ones might simply lean on the disc, or worse, push it in the opposite direction.

When you find people who help you get your disc spinning, it's important to retain them. One of the ways you do that is by regularly evaluating them, then compensating them accordingly.

Continuing education. Our instructors took care of their own certifications, but there were always big conferences coming to Florida. Christi organized groups of instructors to go to these events. She'd make it a fun weekend. A group from our facility would, for example, go to Miami Beach for a convention. Christi went, too. They'd get hotel rooms and all bunk together, which made it as much about connection as education.

When Christi did instructor evaluations, she often gave them money toward continuing education. We required that they give us the receipt, then we reimbursed them. They had to use it within the year, because we didn't want continuing education credit accumulating. We wanted them regularly learning and growing.

In the same mode, when our gymnastics team traveled to meets, Christi often took the group of coaches out to dinner. We gave them a stipend for their meals (and rooms, of course), but when Christi took them out, they didn't have to use their stipend. Christi would pay for that night out, because she wanted to treat them.

Salary or hourly? Some of our gymnastics staff were on salary, as was our general manager. But for the most part, hourly pay made for better accountability. We liked an honest day's work, an honest day's pay, and the ability to clock in and clock out.

Most of our employees were hourly, including the directors. But hourly rates were high, especially for directors. Our dance director, who worked thirty hours a week, had the highest hourly rate in the facility.

GREAT IDEAS

Sometimes, an employee came to us with a new program or a new idea. Even if we liked the idea, that didn't always mean we gave that person license to run with it. We had to ask ourselves if they were the person to see it through. Did they have the energy and commitment to make it work? For some people, ideas are easy to come up with, but implementation takes a different skill set. We never put anyone in charge of something they didn't have the passion to do.

Don (whom we mentioned earlier) is a good example of someone who had a lot of ideas he would throw around. We loved that, because we knew it gave him a sense of ownership. Not all of his ideas were put in place, but we always recognized and appreciated a good idea.

Some of our best business ideas and improvements came from our employees and members. The key to uncovering them, however, is to develop an open culture that encourages everyone's input.

ACCOUNTABILITY

Holding employees accountable is difficult. At first, we worried it would communicate distrust if we continually reminded staff that we held them to a standard. But the reality is, written job descriptions aren't effective if you don't use checks and balances to follow up. Tough conversations yield results.

Honestly, it's the same in any relationship, even a marriage. For years, the two of us shied away from having some tough, but much-needed conversations in our marriage. It caused us to grow apart, and our marriage almost didn't survive it. (More on that in Chapter Nine.)

Being vulnerable enough to have tough discussions is the key to unlocking amazing possibilities—in life and at work. Accountability has to be done, and it only works if it's done together.

NEGATIVE BEHAVIORS

As we grew, our leadership style regarding employee problems changed. In the early years, we didn't want to offend anyone, so we sugarcoated constructive feedback. We'd give feedback to a group, hoping the person who needed to hear it would take heed.

As you could probably guess, usually that person thought the feedback was intended for someone else. So, in years four and five of running the business, we got bold and actually talked with employees one on one. But there was still plenty of sugar, and no real consequences if behavior didn't change.

Eventually, in the middle years, we realized people actually respected us more when we spoke directly and clearly with them. We cited specific examples. We stated our expectations about areas that needed improvement. If warranted, we made sure employees knew they were in jeopardy of losing their position if behavior did not improve.

We also brought in a third person and documented the meeting. Both of these practices helped convey the importance of the issues to be addressed.

COWORKER NEGATIVITY: THREE CHOICES

We always told our staff that if they heard other staff members being negative, they had several choices. One was to simply stay silent. A second was leave the group and take the issue to their manager.

The third choice is the hardest: saying to the group, "I'd rather not talk about that," and then turning the discussion to a positive note.

This is difficult in practice, because when someone is speaking negatively, it's human nature to feel intimidated. We all want to be liked. We might disagree with the negativity, but internally, we're thinking, *if I confront that person, they're not going to like me. They might get others to not like me, either. I'm not going to be included anymore.*

But the truth is, not standing up to negativity allows it to fester, both within one's own spirit and within your company culture.

COMPASSION

We showed compassion in dealing with outside issues, especially when we realized that negativity *at* work often stemmed from issues *outside* of work. But we came to learn that some personality traits are hardwired. Mere "software updates" often aren't enough.

We were building a culture of positivity and encouragement. We knew that if we allowed negative people to remain in this culture, we could lose other, great people.

For that reason, it was important to zero in when someone acted negatively. We reprimanded and, in some cases, there was a consequence. Being direct is always worth it, because it shows care and concern. We gave people a chance to improve. Everyone deserves that.

Sometimes people *can* change, and when they did, we were thankful, both for them and for our culture. That being said, if changes weren't forthcoming and there was continued negativity, the employee usually needed to find another place to work.

GAME CHANGERS

One of the magical parts of life is you don't know who you're going to meet, hire, or connect with during any given day. Throughout our business life, many people came along who made possible what had previously seemed impossible. We'd like to introduce you to a few of them.

Lorraine. Employees who believed in serving others first were an integral part of our success. When a person cares for others, it's a blessing to everyone around them. Lorraine was one of those people. Every day, she demonstrated that she was there for our members. Their happiness was more important to her than her own.

Brian. Running a business is like juggling, walking a tightrope, and making conversation simultaneously—all day long. When you pull it off, it's awesome. But when something breaks down, now you're dodging arrows while you juggle, tightrope-walk, and talk.

Brian caught arrows midair, before they hit us, then slayed the archer who was slinging them. Whether it was electrical, mechanical, or plumbing, Brian could find (or make) the parts to fix the issue. He also constructed walls, built decks, installed windows, renovated bathrooms, and laid acres of flooring throughout the years. Much of his work happened after the doors were locked and the lights should have been out.

Nancy. You know how some people simply make you feel better just by seeing their smiling faces? Nancy was like that. She managed our insurance-based senior fitness program and grew it into one of the largest in the state. Nancy made a point of learning members' names, celebrating birthdays, and scheduling social events for our senior members. These members benefited as much from the community Nancy created as they did from their fitness routines, if not more. They developed friendships that carried on outside the club. While many clubs' senior program classes were given little attention, Nancy mentored her class instructors to make sure we delivered high-quality classes for seniors. She handled issues with class and grace, and she was loved by everyone she encountered. You always felt better after being with Nancy.

Lenore. A volunteer for two decades, Lenore was vital to our success, especially in the early, lean years. Full disclosure: she's Christi's mother. Lenore knew how to make everybody feel special and valued. She's a great listener; she'd remember your kid's name, your dog's name, small details about what was going on with you. The next time you came in, Lenore might say, "How did it go at the doctor's office? How's your son's ear infection?"

Learning people's names is Relationships 101, and it's powerful. Remembering details like Lenore does takes it to a whole other level. When she said, "We're glad you're here," she truly meant it. The warmth she brought to our business was palpable.

There are many others who could be mentioned. We were blessed to have so many staff members give of themselves and serve our community.

LEADING THE LEADERS

When you start a business, you run every area yourself. As the business grows, more departments become necessary, with managers to run them. Developing them as leaders is one of the best ways to show you care about them.

Initially, our leadership development was one on one, helping managers handle difficult situations and make decisions about their department's direction. While helpful, this doesn't give managers the ability to build confidence and learn from their mistakes.

Within a year of relocating to the new building, our membership and staff almost doubled. As we hired additional managers and gave them more responsibility, we also implemented monthly leadership meetings.

The initial goal was to develop connections as the gym grew and everyone became busier in their day-to-day work. Over the next few years, the meetings became more structured. The two of us would present highlights of a chapter from one of the management books that resonated with us. We asked the group how they might implement these principles in their departments. Later, they'd report back about how a concept was received, and if they foresaw long-term benefits.

The difficulty with a regular monthly meeting (besides increasing payroll) is keeping people engaged. You do not want passive participation in such events. Sometimes, we held lunch meetings at new restaurants in town. We'd discuss the business positives and negatives we noticed firsthand. That kept things more interesting.

Later, we began assigning a book chapter each month to a different leader. Just as we'd done, their responsibility was to read the chapter in advance of the meeting and present what they gleaned from it. This was a great way to get them out of their comfort zones and working on presentation and communication skills. This process also helped us discern whether an individual was growing as a leader. Many of them would feel nervous when it was their time to present a chapter. But after they got through it, we were all drawn closer together. Vulnerability is a catalyst to building deeper relationships.

THE BEST NON-COMPETE

The best non-compete is to create an environment where people don't want to work somewhere else.

When people know you care, they put more of themselves into what they do. When our employees were approached by other health club owners to teach classes for them, they weren't eager to leave us. That was true even if they were being offered more money to work somewhere else.

Why? Because at our gym, they were more than just instructors. They were part of an organization that invested in people. Christi's yearly evaluations are a great example of that. The yearly review helped instructors become better at their craft. At the same time, it built strong relationships within the team.

We would hear of other clubs telling instructors, "If you teach for us, you can't teach anywhere else." We never did that, but they stayed with us anyway. When your staff sticks around, it's a sign of loyalty. It's a sign that employees feel like they belong.

MEET AN EMPLOYEE: DON'S STORY

Steve and Christi had a unique ability to see an individual's talents and gifts. I started out in 2013 as the welcome-desk manager, and after a few years, I became the general manager. I remember Steve saying one of the reasons they offered me the general manager job was because, "It's smart to bring in someone who can do the job better than you."

Steve told me that in me, they saw somebody who could be a general manager at a young age. Steve said that I "acted like an owner from day one." Rather than feeling threatened by that, he saw it as a positive character trait of mine.

Christi always had a big smile on her face. She'd take the time to talk. She was calm, pleasant, and wise.

I learned so much while working at Christi's Fitness. The most important lessons I learned were about relationships. I saw how the Wades genuinely cared about people and put that into practice. They didn't see people as dollar signs. They taught me that if you're focusing on people, the financial thing often takes care of itself.

The Wades said that when you have the right people in the right positions, there's more time to be creative. If I went to them with an idea, they wanted to know how much it would cost. I'll be honest—I came up with some grandiose ideas! They'd remind me to bring it back down to earth.

One idea they let me run with was to paint all the concrete car stops in the parking lot. I painted them with words like, "Humility," "Gratitude," and "Forgiveness." The idea was that members could park in front of the word that resonated for them or would inspire them that day.

Often, a member would come in and tell me what word they'd parked by and how much it meant to them, in their life at that moment. "It's exactly what I needed to hear today," they'd say.

For me, "Humility" always stuck out. Seeing that word daily reminded me that it's not all about me.

Steve and Christi would say, "Guys, we're in this together. The success of the club is in working as a team." The leadership meetings were an example of that. When you discuss a specific topic from a management book in a room full of leaders, people bring their varied experiences and skills to the table. We all learned from each other.

The Wades wouldn't ask someone to do something if they weren't willing to do it themselves. So, if I ended up scrubbing toilets at work, I was humbled by that, but I knew I wasn't alone. We were a team.

I was challenged more at that job than at any other in my life, except running my own business. Not because the Wades were difficult to work for, but because of the challenges they entrusted to me. Overcoming those challenges helped me grow.

Steve absolutely could have done my job. But he'd say, "Now it's your turn to do it." We became good friends. I never wanted to let the guy down.

About a year after Christi's Fitness was sold, I left to start my own fitness facility, Element. My business partner, Tisha, is also a former Christi's employee. I know Steve and Christi enjoyed seeing their former employees striking out on their own, using what they'd learned while working at Christi's.

The Wades taught me about "finding the right people to put on the bus." Tisha was one of those people. While I was the welcome-desk manager at Christi's, she was a member. I noticed her energy and enthusiasm. One day, I chased her down in the parking lot.

"Are you looking for a job?" I asked.

"Not really," she said. "But what do you have in mind?"

I told her I needed an extra welcome-desk team member. Within a few years, Tisha was the assistant manager of Christi's Fitness.

After the business was sold, the two of us worked closely together to help transition to the new ownership.

When I worked at Christi's Fitness, my reason for working hard was not to get a promotion or make more money. I worked hard because Steve and Christi cared about me and believed in me. In return, I wanted to give them my absolute best.

ELEVATE THE ORDINARY

- How can you align your core values with making smart business decisions?
- In business, you have to figure out how to differentiate yourself. What will make the way you run your business stand out from your competition?
- What kinds of people do you want to hire? Do you want employees similar to yourself? Are you more concerned with character or skill set?
- In what ways can you show appreciation for your employees? How can you get creative with employee appreciation?
- When things don't go well, are you prepared to be direct with employees?
- As your company grows, how will you hire managers and delegate responsibilities? Once managers are on board, how will you help them develop and grow?
- How will you give employees a sense of ownership in your business? What will motivate great employees to stay with you, instead of going somewhere else?

CHAPTER FIVE

BUILDING A CULTURE, PART TWO: MEMBERS

MISSION STATEMENT—AGAIN

Our mission, as stated, was, "To make the fitness experience an inspiration for the families of our community.

A key concept of this statement is that *members and families come first.* We did that simply because we believe it's the right thing to do. But the ripple effect is, it makes for good business. When you treat customers right, other aspects of your business tend to come together more easily.

HONEST AND FAIR PRICING

To provide members with the experience we wanted them to have, we invested in the right staff and in our facilities. In order to make these investments and operate the club as our members deserved, we knew what we needed to charge for membership.

Christi's Fitness eventually became the most expensive independent health club in our area. There were other businesses offering fitness programs: resorts, boutique fitness places like Orangetheory, private yoga studios, and so on. Those might cost more than belonging to our club, but in terms of full fitness facilities, we were the most expensive in Vero Beach.

Did we do this because we were focused, above all else, on making a buck? Quite the contrary. Our goal was to *retain* members—and we knew we couldn't do that by giving a discount one day, then jacking up our prices the next.

Gyms are notorious for negotiating rates with prospective members. It's the industry model, but we never did that. Even in the middle of the 2008 recession, we kept our rates consistent. We told prospective members, "This is the rate. We'd love to have you here, and your fee will be the posted rate."

That being said, we did offer specials once a year. In January (a time when many people decide to join a gym), we might waive the registration fee for the first two weeks of the month. And we offered some corporate packages, for all of the staff of a particular company, for example. But overall, we used consistent pricing.

We knew that in targeting an upscale membership, we had to provide services that were in balance with our pricing. Our members were willing to pay our rate because they knew our services were well worth it.

MEMBER RETENTION

IHRSA (International Health, Racquet & Sportsclub Association) was the leading fitness industry organization we belonged to and accessed frequently for continuing education and conferences. They stated in an online article written in 2018 regarding retention, "*Member retention may now form the lifeblood to a club's bottom line.*" We knew there was great benefit to retaining members, rather than having them come and go. With that in mind, we spent time developing strategies and policies that not only caused members to stick around, but also motivated them to recommend our gym to others. Word of mouth is the best advertising out there, and we wanted as much of it as possible.

We developed a few basic strategies that helped with member retention. It took some time to finesse, but below are some of the policies that worked for us.

No increase to existing members' rates. As with any business, we had to increase rates over time. The cost of doing business goes up; that's just a reality in most industries, including ours. That being said, our policy was, as long as a member didn't cancel their membership, they retained the membership rate they'd originally signed up with. It was a tangible way of saying thank you for being with us for so many years.

Shelley, a member you'll meet later in this chapter, belonged to our gym for twenty years. As such, she had a very low rate. In all those years, she never let her membership lapse, which provided her with a great price for her membership.

For us, there was non-monetary value in having someone like Shelley at our club for twenty years. She referred countless people to the club. How many positive comments do you think she made about us? How many staff members did she get to know? How many other members became her friends?

Compassion. If someone had a surgery or some type of illness and they couldn't participate at the club temporarily, we medically extended their agreement. We didn't charge them while they were unable to come to the gym. This was a bit complicated to administer, but it demonstrated compassion, and members appreciated it. Not only that, but they spread the word to other members and prospective members about this policy. It showed that we put customers first, before the dollar.

Electronic Funds Transfer (EFT). As mentioned earlier, we began using EFT soon after opening our club. Members could sign up for EFT or pay in full, in advance. We didn't offer other payment options. This streamlined the administrative side for us, and also helped ensure a steady cash flow. We made sure prospective members knew in advance how EFT worked. There were no surprises, and most people came on board with it fairly easily. To build trust with our members, we handled our billing carefully. We protected their private account information and corrected any mistakes in a timely manner, which further built trust and our reputation in the community.

SETTING OURSELVES APART FROM THE COMPETITION

We chose to distance ourselves as far from the low-cost gym model as we could. This, in turn, helped us develop a membership base that could afford to continue paying our rates monthly—which, over time, gave us a stable financial base. We wanted to attract members who could afford personal training, massage, an additional membership for their spouse, or gymnastics for their child. Eventually, we targeted an average household annual income of $75,000 and up.

We became the club with the highest revenue and profit in Vero Beach. What could be better than that? Well, to be honest, our daughter won her high school basketball state championship, and our son became a pastor. (Sorry, little parental brag moment there. Life's most treasured moments are not always about business!)

But back to business. What did we do to set ourselves apart? A few ideas follow.

The personal touch. We had a photograph of our family—Christi, Steve, and our kids—in the front entrance. Throughout the years, we updated the photo. Our kids were babies when the first picture went up. Over the years, as the photo changed, members watched our kids grow. People always got a kick out of it when a new Wade family photo went up.

Eventually, our club became large enough that we didn't know every member personally. And yet, members knew what *we* looked like, because of the photo. If they wanted to find us, they knew who to look for.

The message the family photo gave members was, "We're showing you who we are. If you need us, we're here for you." It enhanced our brand as a family business you could trust.

A sincere thank you. If a member had been with us long term, and (for whatever reason) they discontinued their membership, Steve would either write them a letter or call them, simply to thank them for all their years of supporting our business. He didn't try to talk them into staying. He just thanked them for choosing us and being a member.

There's always going to be a payoff to that. Again, it goes back to your business's reputation in the community. What are people saying about you? When you reach out to someone personally like this (without a monetary incentive), they'll say good things.

There were even some members who hardly came to the gym at all, yet retained their memberships. Often, we learned they did this simply because they wanted to support us. They believed in what we were doing.

Online reviews. With the ability to post a review online, customers have incredible leverage over businesses. For this reason, it's vital to be proactive about customer care and service.

If a member had a complaint, we did our best to address it *before* they posted a bad review. Whether it was a membership issue or a piece of equipment, it was much better to spend a few hundred dollars taking care of their concern than to have to deal with a bad online review. We looked at it as marketing money well spent.

MEMBER APPRECIATION EVENTS

Showing appreciation for our members was a large part of what set us apart from the low-cost clubs. Over the years, we developed a variety of events to show appreciation.

Member appreciation parties. For many years, we organized a member appreciation party once a year. Members had the option to be a part of it, or they could just do their normal workout. It was up to them.

We scheduled live musicians for classes. In group exercise classes, two instructors would team up to teach, so they could feed off each other's energy. Sometimes, instructors dressed up and made it themed. One year, we hired a drummer to drum along with the music in step class. The idea was to mix things up, make it feel special and unique.

We set up games and raffles. Many times, we hired a DJ or an acoustic guitar player/singer to be in the weight room. He emceed contests and played music, which gave a distinct energy to the weight room on that day. We coordinated with our trainers to, for example, recruit people for a plank contest. Six or seven members would be holding plank, with the DJ counting their time aloud. The member who held plank longest could spin the wheel and get a prize. A few members said it was too loud, but 95% of them loved it.

We had food and drinks. In the morning, we'd have coffee, bagels, and fruit. Throughout the day, we'd offer other food items. We'd ask members and staff if they had a healthy recipe they liked, and if they'd be willing to make that dish for the party. If they shared the recipe with us, we'd print copies and place them next to the dish. People like sharing something they've made.

One time, early on, we rented a different venue. Our membership appreciation party that year was a 1960s/1970s theme, and everybody dressed up. That was memorable!

Valentine's Day. For many years, Christi-and-Steve team taught a Valentine's Day cycling class. We encouraged members to bring spouses or significant others to the class. We'd do "fun facts" games to help people get to know each other, with prizes. One year, we set it up in three rooms, with three different types of classes. At that point, we had a marketing team comprised of young adults, led by Don and another staff member, Rachel (whom you'll meet in a later chapter). We set it up in the spin room, the main studio, and the gymnastics room (but we made gymnastics playful and fun for adults). Afterwards, there was fancy chocolate, donated by a local shop, as well as wine. Everyone loved celebrating with wine and chocolate!

Gymnastics "mini-meets" and other events. For the gymnastics program, we held "mini-meets." The beginner gymnasts put on a show for their parents, grandparents, and others. This gave these beginners a feel for what it was like to be in a gymnastics meet. Awards were given, and it was special for everyone.

On other days, we scheduled times when parents could come in the gymnastics room and video their children's skills, as a keepsake for years to come. We also had gymnasts and dancers participate in festivals in the community that encouraged performances from area programs like ours.

Dads' Day. For this event, fathers of preschool gymnasts joined the class. Most of the time, it was moms bringing their kids to class, so to have dads come was a big deal. Each kid was proud to show their dad what they could do, and they loved to laugh at him when he tried. For a four-year-old, watching your dad swing on the bars or try to balance as he walked across a four-inch-wide beam was hilarious. Steve worried that one of those guys would pull something. That never happened, but there were always a few sore dads the next day!

We held Dads' Day on a weekend, when we normally didn't have classes. Eventually, there were 120 kids in our preschool program, so the event became large. It was open to every preschooler and dad, but they had to sign up in advance to participate.

Family Fun Day. This was a fun day for everyone. We hired face painters and someone to make balloons. One of our staff, who was also in acting school, dressed up as a princess from *Frozen*, which was a big hit with the kids.

We seldom charged for any of our events. They were simply a way to thank members for their support and to demonstrate a creative, fun side to the business. Events took time, planning, organization, and payroll. We spent money to have events, but not a lot. The things that make the most difference usually don't cost too much money.

Businesses are always looking for the next big thing to bolster their bottom line, but they might be looking in the wrong areas. Often, it's as basic and simple as connecting with people and developing relationships. The return on investment was that everyone walked away with stronger connections, great memories, and positive feelings about our business. And that's priceless!

KEEPING THEIR KIDS HAPPY

We knew that if kids wanted to come to our facility, parents would continue to come, too. We made sure to create an environment that truly welcomed families and children.

A unique experience. Not every kid took classes. Some were too young, or else they wanted to just play while their parents took a class. So we made sure the babysitting room provided a truly unique experience. We had a saltwater tank, and kids loved to watch the fish. We had a dress-up box full of costumes. There were crafts and story times.

At one point, we revamped the whole babysitting room. As mentioned in the previous chapter, we called it the Kids' Kingdom. It was themed like an Old English kingdom. Steve built a two-story castle, and we had a wallscape with characters painted on it.

We kept the babysitting room spotless. Our babysitters were expected to clean any time there were only a few kids in the room, or when all the kids were playing happily on their own.

We worked to keep our babysitting staff happy, and many of them stayed with us for years. We kept the babysitting room overstaffed; we preferred having too many staff and not enough kids to the other way around. Members didn't need to sign up to use the babysitting room; it was drop in. At any given time, there could be ten kids or thirty kids. We didn't want to overwhelm staff, so we made sure there were always enough workers during peak times.

Charging for babysitting. We charged twenty dollars a month per child for babysitting. No other health club in our area charged for babysitting, but other clubs pretty much hoped few members would use their babysitting room. They put very little importance on it and had minimal staff. We had a reputation for great babysitting, so people were willing to pay that small amount for it. Our message was that kids' well-being is at the top of our list.

We knew having great staff in our babysitting room cost us more than we billed for monthly babysitting fees. But there were residual benefits later. Children who spent time in the babysitting room became comfortable in the facility and would often go on to join our structured children's programs. This demonstrates how a loss leader in one area can pay off in the long run—and add to your brand and culture along the way.

GROUP EXERCISE CLASSES

No matter what type of business you're in, there will inevitably be occasional moments when you disappoint customers. In our business, sometimes that meant cancelled classes. We worked hard to ensure classes weren't cancelled. If an instructor didn't show up, oftentimes we were able to recruit someone from our staff to fill in until another instructor (or the one that was supposed to teach) was able to get there and take over.

Of course, that wasn't ideal. The key is to minimize the frequency of such moments, and when they do happen, to handle them with understanding and grace.

Make allies, not enemies. We realized if we handled tough situations like cancelled classes the right way, we could make allies instead of enemies. On the rare occasion when we had to cancel a class, the welcome-desk staff recorded all the names of all members who showed up for the class. Sometimes, we gave them a logo item, such as a towel or water bottle. Or we made up a little coupon for a drink or snack from our pro shop.

No matter what else we did, we always sent a handwritten note, apologizing for the inconvenience. One time, for a 6:00 a.m. no-show, the entire group received Starbucks gift cards in their letters. People had pulled themselves out of bed to get to class. They'd created their whole schedule for the day, starting bright and early with a workout. Nobody wants to get up in the dark, get to the gym, and then learn the instructor didn't show up. It's not a minor thing, and we wanted to recognize that.

Even at a later time, like 8:30 or 9:00 in the morning, it was a big deal. We knew what it was like to be a busy parent in the morning—packing lunches, getting the crying baby in the car, getting your older kids to school, going into the babysitting room and peeling a clinging child off your leg. You get through all that and you're ready for your class, your moment of sanity for the day. And then you get to the door of the group exercise room and the instructor's a no-show? What a terrible disappointment.

The most important thing wasn't the gift card or the coupon or the towel. It was the acknowledgement that we'd inconvenienced them, and we were truly sorry.

How many to run a class? In our industry, many clubs will have a "number." For example, if there aren't at least five people at class start time, then class is cancelled.-

We always thought that was a poor business practice. Our number was one. If only one person showed up, we still ran the class. The instructor was paid, and many times the member enjoyed a private "group" class. Sometimes, the member declined, saying we didn't need to bother—which was fine; it was up to them. But even then, the instructor was paid. Those situations showed our staff and members that we were serious about how much every person mattered.

Cancellations affect instructors, too. Christi knew, because she also was an instructor, what it takes to plan and execute a class. Instructors had to have their music and their program prepared. They had to drive over to the club and be ready to teach.

When clubs tell an instructor that their class is cancelled because of low turnout, and then they don't pay the instructor, that instructor has wasted time and energy. That's bound to create resentment.

We never wanted that to happen. We wanted our instructors to trust us and know we valued them. If they were scheduled to teach and they showed up to teach, we paid them for their time.

That said, we were always evaluating class popularity. If a particular class frequently had low turnout, it was time for Christi to make a change to the programming for that class.

PREPARING MEMBERS FOR CHANGE

We lived by the motto of change. We knew that in order to maintain our goal of being the best quality high-end club in our area, we had to continually make changes to stay ahead of our competition.

When a change was coming, we made it a priority to prep members. When it comes as an abrupt surprise, even if you get positive feedback overall, some people will inevitably be upset. We alleviated a lot of that by making members a part of a change.

Our biggest change by far was going from the rental space to purchasing and developing a new commercial space of our own. As the new facility was being developed, we had a lot of time to talk with members about it. We did a survey, asking them what they'd like to see in the new facility. We built our new facility based on members' dreams and wants for their ideal fitness facility.

Moving to the new space meant our costs would go up, which, in turn, meant we'd have to charge more. This was the only time we did a price increase for *existing* members. As noted earlier, as long as a member kept their membership active, their rate stayed the same. This was true for all the years we were in business, with the singular exception of when we moved to the new facility. We prepped them for this price increase about a month before it happened. By then, the new building was nearly finished, and they could see—it was right across the street, after all—how wonderful the new space was going to be. That made it easier for them to acknowledge the need for a rate increase.

"PUTTING OUT THE FIRE": RESPONDING WHEN DISASTER STRIKES

During about our fifth year in the rented space, the kitchen of a restaurant in our plaza, connected to our building, caught fire. Smoke poured into the gym. We received a call at three in the morning from the fire department, and Steve headed straight to the gym.

The fire was put out with no physical damage to our space, but we had smoke damage throughout the whole gym. It created a strong odor that persisted for weeks.

We tried everything to get rid of the smell. We set up fans and changed all the filters. We cleaned the carpets and wiped down the walls. We changed out all the acoustic ceiling tiles. We felt like we were doing everything we could to make the smell go away, but it persisted. We repainted. We rescrubbed the carpets. We just kept at it.

Eventually, we hired a smoke restoration company. They brought in ozone machines and wiped down all the walls again. They steam-cleaned the carpets. Still, the smell lingered.

Nothing seemed to help but the passage of time. Eventually, after about three months, the smell finally went away.

In all that time, we never closed the club. A staff member, Lorraine (whom you met in the previous chapter), took it upon herself to set up a table in the parking lot and talk to members before they went in. She'd greet them and tell them what had happened, so they were prepared before they went inside. They could venture into the building to see if they could handle the smell or not.

Some members were able to deal with it, but a lot of them weren't. But even those members knew we were doing everything we could to rectify the situation. Our members saw how we were in the trenches, taking every step possible to make things better.

This is what customers want to see when there's a problem of any kind. People know that problems arise. Unforeseen circumstances can happen to anyone. The key is in how you, as the business owner, handle the issue.

We could have closed, filed an insurance claim, and waited until the work was done. But our response showed something different: a willingness to go to extreme lengths to minimize disruption to the services that members were counting on and had paid for.

It took time, money, and patience. Some staff stayed long into the evening with Steve, working on mitigation. That meant extra payroll during that time, but it was worth it.

THE IMPORTANCE OF LISTENING—AND ACTING ON WHAT YOU HEAR

Once we were in the new facility, we had a member suggestion board, built by Steve. It was a large, four-sided, standing tower that we set up near the welcome desk. Members could post a suggestion for others to read. This was an idea from a consultant, Thomas Plummer, who held conferences and wrote books for the fitness industry.

Our responses to each suggestion were on the board, too. Even if we were not going to make the change the member suggested, we responded with a note explaining why.

It's important to mention that we kept the negative comments up and responded to those, too. If it was something like, "The bathroom was dirty," our response was, "We're so sorry. We'll get on that as soon as possible. We strive to be the cleanest club in town."

The exception was a mean-spirited comment about a specific person. We didn't allow members to publicly attack anyone. If that happened, we took down the note and addressed the issue privately.

At one point, we added four tiled, 55-inch TVs to the weight room to make a large video screen. The software allowed us to program the video and photo content on the screen, so we put the suggestions and our responses there, too. People could read them while working out. This demonstrated we were serious about getting member suggestions and feedback.

LET PEOPLE HAVE THEIR SAY

If staff heard about a member being disgruntled, they usually brought it to Steve, who would then talk with that member. Christi says, "Steve is great at reading people and being able to calm a situation. He's diplomatic. As humans, our instinct is to be defensive, but Steve never let a situation at the club escalate. Without receiving fire in return, the other person's tone began to drop almost immediately."

Steve concurs. "What I'd do is remain silent while they spoke, even if they were yelling. If you're just nodding and looking someone in the eye, you're not ignoring them but you're not getting into an argument, either. Eventually, they began to hear how out of control they sounded, how unreasonable they were being. Some would apologize before I said a single word."

Another great technique is to be ready with paper and pen. Steve would say, "I want to make sure I get this down, so we can address the issue." Suddenly, the words someone uses become a little different, because it's being recorded. That helps de-escalate things, and it also provides a concrete record, which is useful for follow-through. Steve got their name and phone number, and he made a point of keeping in touch about the issue.

The core issue is communication. The reality is, most of us are busy and often feel disconnected from others. So many conflicts arise from a lack of communication, a lack of true connection between people.

LISTENING WORKS IN OTHER RELATIONSHIPS, TOO

Let's say you've got a customer who's disgruntled, but most of your other customers are very happy. In this scenario, some business owners might think, *I don't need to address that. It's an isolated incident, and it will blow over.* Maybe it will, but in our experience, it's a mistake to ignore it.

The same could be said for any relationship, not just a business one. Suppose, in a marriage like ours, where two people are not only married but are also business partners, you agree on how to raise the kids, how to spend the money, and what works for most business issues. All great, right?

But suppose you're not connecting intimately as a couple. You might think, *but those other things are great, so that one thing will take care of itself.*

The answer in this scenario is exactly the same as it is for the sole disgruntled customer. No matter how difficult, it's important to confront uncomfortable situations. If you communicate with compassion in your heart and truth in your words, you show the other person that you care. Moreover, you demonstrate the importance of the situation not just for the two people involved, but for the good of the entire community—whether that community is a business, a family, or any other group of people bound by relationships.

EVERY CONFRONTATION TEACHES A LESSON

Listening to staff and members can be difficult. Actually, listening to anyone is hard. In general, we only like to listen if the information presented is compatible with our thinking. If not, while someone else is talking, often we're formulating our (possibly quite opinionated) response.

Especially as business owners, we completely understand this. When you're working fourteen-hour days and trying to do the best job you can, it's natural to become defensive about a complaint. You might not even realize you're taking it personally.

But what we learned in all our years of business is that there's something to discover in every confrontation. We improved our customer service significantly because of member and staff complaints. We also had a few good laughs along the way! And we shared in them together.

LET'S WIN

Have you ever been around a kids' sporting event? If you have, you'll probably agree that some sports parents are really irritating. And in some ways, it's understandable. You want that win *so* bad for your child.

Or is it for you? When a parent yells at the referee, are they really helping their kid's team? Usually, that parent ends up embarrassing their child and annoying the officials.

The same elements of restraint apply in business. We made sure our staff knew to never make a negative comment about a competitor, even if a potential member was heaping insults on that competitor.

During the recession, a Planet Fitness opened half a mile away from our gym. There was also another 55,000-square foot club within one mile. Within a five-mile radius, there were several personal training gyms, a few boutique fitness studios, two 24-hour gyms, and a large all-women's facility. The competition was fierce, but we kept our focus on treating people well.

Anytime a business criticizes a competitor to get ahead, they end up losing. We knew that, and we instructed our staff, "Don't engage in that conversation. Exercise self-control." We told them to stay positive and simply say, "We're just glad you're here."

That's how you win.

THE IMPORTANCE OF PATIENCE—AND FOLLOWING THROUGH

A tool that's important to use is patience. For instance, when a member approached Steve with a complaint that he initially found a bit over the top, Steve's response was, "Let me think about it and get back to you tomorrow."

In all honesty, we were taken back a few times by people who seemed to live in a vacuum. They would come at us hard and not let up. Listening first was our mantra, but it's tough when someone is breathing fire on you.

Regardless, one thing was true of almost every unruly member: the source of their anger was really another situation or circumstance in their life. Over time, we began to understand this and have more empathy for them. We realized that no one is at their best 100% of the time. Once that realization was made, things got easier. We just did our best to put ourselves in their shoes and follow through regarding their issue.

Sometimes, by the time Steve got back to them, they'd come to this realization, too. They might have calmed down enough to see that fit they threw actually stemmed from another issue in their life, and resolving the specifics became easier.

We didn't resolve every problem, but we were consistent in our approach to these situations. We're only as clean as our dirtiest corner in the building. You're only as trustworthy as the number of times you follow through on your word.

"When people can't agree, it's often because there is no empathy, no sense of shared experience. If you feel what others feel, you're more likely to see what they see. Then you can understand each other. Then you can move to the honest and respectful exchange of ideas that is a mark of successful partnership."
– Melinda Gates

CREATING AN EXPERIENCE

Creating an experience for customers starts with culture and ends with perception. Facilities and customer service are sandwiched between.

The experience starts before a customer even drives into your parking lot or walks up to your business. What's your reputation in the community? What do online reviews say?

Once a potential customer arrives at your business, is parking readily available? What does the outside of your building look like? The signage and the grounds? Is there trash around? Is the entrance area clean?

All that happens before they step foot in the door. The stage has to be set!

One of the ways we set our stage was those encouraging words that our employee, Don, painted on our concrete parking space stops. (He talked about these in the previous chapter.) Some members said it would change their mindset for the day. A few would even drive around looking for the right word to express how they felt that day.

Culture continues when someone walks in your door. If the culture is right, your customers will feel it the moment they walk in. It won't matter which staff person greets them, because a unified culture is apparent everywhere. Customers can't escape it, and they want to come back, even if they can't articulate why.

For a visitor, the first indication of our brand was a ten-foot-high by thirty-foot-long, high-resolution wallscape of the beach. It spanned the curved wall behind our front desk. The spacious entry layout created a welcoming atmosphere and kept the weight room out of initial view. This floor plan helped potential members feel comfortable in what might otherwise be an intimidating environment for the non-exerciser.

In our weight room, our large video wall played clips of people traveling all over the world—walking, hiking, biking, running, skydiving, surfing, and so on. These were professionally made videos we accessed through a digital media company. It cost $400 per month, but really set us apart from an experience standpoint. Every video showed an outdoor event. We wanted our members to make the connection that fitness indoors can prepare you for enjoying the world outdoors.

Outside the gymnastics area, we had a large LED TV with a real-time, rolling schedule of kids' classes and their location within the gym. We could update the software for any schedule changes and add promotional marketing of our other children's programs. The digital media company custom-programmed this for our facility. This fit in with our premium brand and put us a level above the competition.

One time, a member told Steve that there were too many light fixtures in our ceiling. The member suggested we take out every other bulb to save on electricity. It sounded like a good idea, until Steve did it. The atmosphere changed, it wasn't as bright. So, Steve replaced all the bulbs with upgraded "daylight" bulbs, which made it feel like sunshine inside.

BEING PRESENT

As our business grew, so did the challenges we faced every day. If we went to the club hoping to accomplish a scheduled list of tasks, most times we left feeling as though we'd wasted our day. All day long, we were handling people problems and helping others make decisions. That's valid work, but it meant the scheduled work got sidelined. We learned that desk work needed to be done at home, and our expectations for time at the gym had to be adjusted.

There's no substitute for being present with your staff and customers. It's taxing and time consuming, but it builds high-value trust. It shows customers how much you care. And for your staff, it models true leadership.

Staff can put out some fires for you, but many problems require a level of authority they haven't earned. Members want to know leadership is listening and will take action. Employees want the assurance that leadership will back them up or stand in the gap when needed.

It's impossible to accomplish those vital elements of leadership if you're not present. People are counting on you, and as a business owner or general manager, you *need* to be there for them.

MEET A MEMBER: SHELLEY'S STORY

I knew Christi prior to the opening of her club. I took classes with her at other clubs around here. Christi always had tons of energy. The minute she went out on her own, we all went right with her.

That's why I started coming to Christi's. Why did I stay? Because I felt comfortable. It was fun. They offered everything I wanted in a club, and I felt like I was part of the family. Christi's mom, Lenore, worked at the front desk, and she greeted you like family. Everyone looked forward to seeing her each day.

I admire Christi. Besides being a businessperson, she's a great instructor. She explains things so well, anybody can jump in and take a class with her. Her music is great.

The feeling she gave off was that anybody could be successful there, regardless of gender, capabilities, how much you weighed, what you wore. None of that mattered. If you were there, Christi would help you meet your fitness goals.

Other members feel like family as well. Going to the club is my social time. To this day, some of my closest friends are people I met through the gym.

I loved the inspirational words on the parking stops. They were uplifting statements, but they gave you something to think about, too.

My membership fee is worth every dime. It isn't just the physical workout; it's also beneficial for my mental health. I still go every morning, Monday through Friday. I like dance, circuit, and step. I find taking a class fun and energetic. I like someone telling me what to do, choreographing or constructing a class, and putting music with it.

In Vero Beach, people know Christi's by reputation, especially moms, because of the children's programs. The children's programs were so strong, all the moms in town knew about them.

When my daughters were little, they enjoyed the kids' programs. My older daughter, Amanda, started working at Christi's a few hours a week when she was in high school. That led to working summer camps, which led to coaching gymnastics and cheerleading.

After she graduated college, Amanda moved back to Vero Beach, and Steve and Christi offered her a job. For several years, she did marketing for them, taught children's dance, and coached cheerleading.

The lowest time in my life was when I was diagnosed with cancer. I had chemo and lost my hair. I don't know what I'd have done without Christi, Steve, and their gym. They got me through the worst period of my life. During that terrible time, except on the very roughest days, I made myself stay on a routine, which meant getting out of bed and going to the gym. I was so proud of myself for that. Physically, I did it—I made it to classes! But it made me feel better mentally, too.

The club was upscale, yet comfortable. I never felt self-conscious, being there with a scarf covering my head. Everyone was so supportive of me during that time.

I own a jewelry store, Cousineau Jewelers. At my store, we sell literal hearts of gold, but having a figurative heart of gold is vital when you're dealing with people in your business life. Christi and Steve embody that.

ELEVATE THE ORDINARY

- How can you ensure that your product or service lives up to the price you charge for it? It starts with quality, but the more you develop your brand by building relationships and trust, the more you can charge.
- In what ways can you focus on your long-term goals, rather than on your eagerness to generate a short-term profit?
- Will you host special events? If so, what kind? How will you plan for them, while still running your day-to-day business?
- What if the unexpected happens (like smoke damage, a hurricane, or a pandemic)? How will you manage your personal stress over the issue, while at the same time being cognizant of employee and customer needs?
- How do you feel about confrontation? If you're not confident in handling confrontation in a way that will result in positives for you and your business, can you role-play with

a business partner or spouse? Doing so will help you develop skills in this area.

- Do you have definable objectives for your company's culture? In what ways can you improve your physical space to reflect your culture? Remember to pay attention to natural and artificial light sources, ceiling height and acoustics, wall color, cleanliness, and other physical features. Make sure your facility is an appealing space that also demonstrates your culture.

CHAPTER SIX

THE DRIVE TO IMPROVE

LEARNING IS AN INVESTMENT

Learning is investing in yourself, and in your business. During the years we owned the club, our goal was to continually learn, improve, and be open to change.

Part of being the best health club in our area meant going further than the competition. It meant identifying and spending money on important aspects of our business, being creative, and learning about what was coming next in our industry, so we could be the first to bring it to the community.

Some of the innovations we were the first to introduce in our area included nationally known guest presenters, indoor cycling classes, Powerboarding, Group Power (Body Pump style classes), TRX suspension training, and Tribe Team Training™. When we brought in group exercise presenters, we opened it up to the whole community, to bring people together.

Whenever possible, we tried to be first with a fitness trend. We saw it as part of being the best club in our area.

THE IDEA IS NOT ENOUGH

We loved that we had bright, enthusiastic staff, many of whom came to us with great ideas. But one thing we learned was that if someone suggested a new program, even if we loved the idea, we had to think carefully about whether that staff member was the right person to see it through. We realized that in certain instances, the "idea person" wasn't the best "implementation person."

In some cases, even if the idea was great, there was *no* appropriate "implementation person." Sometimes, we simply didn't have the right staffing fit for an idea.

We declined new concepts and programs if we didn't have the right people to lead them. Starting small-group aerial yoga or growing a larger boys' gymnastics program sound like terrific ideas, but only if you have the right managerial staff for a program. If not, the program won't last, and/or it strains other managerial staff.

By the time we sold the business, we were running over 100 group exercise classes a week. We had water aerobics, tai chi, barre class, and a wide variety of "boutique" offerings that we were able to adequately staff and that members enjoyed.

LEARNING FROM OTHERS

As mentioned earlier, Christi worked for Athletics and Fitness Association of America (AFAA), which is one of the largest fitness certification organizations in the country. Initially, Christi was trained to help administer AFAA exams and help with the practical portion of their exams. Later, she was trained as a consultant. For twelve years, she traveled around the country, going into clubs to administer AFAA certifications and present workshops for continuing fitness industry education.

It was weekend work. After we had kids, Christi reduced it even more, to a weekend every month or two. She already had a full schedule, and she didn't want to spend a lot of time doing AFAA work at that point. She'd been working for AFAA before we opened Christi's (and pre-kids), and she began administering AFAA certifications after we opened the club. She continued for about a year after we built our new facility. By then, Christi's Fitness had doubled in size, and our children were a bit older and involved in a lot of activities. Christi wanted more time with our kids, so she stopped working for AFAA.

The dozen years she spent doing this work gave Christi a base for training our club's exercise instructors, as well as an up-close view of what worked and what didn't in other clubs. Christi spent time in all kinds of clubs around the country, meeting and talking with hundreds of people in the industry. At each club, she'd pull schedules, rate sheets, and other information. She'd get ideas for what she liked and wanted to emulate, as well as what we might do differently at our own club.

We did the same thing when we went on vacation. Whenever possible, we'd find a health club to work out at. We wouldn't necessarily introduce ourselves as club owners, but instead went in as guests, to get a feel for what the experience was like for someone walking in off the street.

Learning how other clubs functioned was always helpful. We also learned a lot about customer service from other industries. Whenever a new restaurant opened in Vero Beach, we always tried to check it out. As mentioned earlier, sometimes we'd have a staff meeting in a restaurant. We'd get to see what their customer service was like, and we used it as a teaching moment for our staff.

We also gained much knowledge at fitness conferences. These conferences exposed us to new ideas with the potential to impact our business. The difficulty is, you don't know which ideas will work with your staff and your local market. Generally, we might implement one or two concepts we learned about at a conference, ideas that worked with our culture and for which we had appropriate staffing.

WHAT OUR INDUSTRY TOLD US (AND WHY WE IGNORED THIS ADVICE)

Our industry said we had to develop profit centers. We were told to "focus on dollars per member." We were urged to use tools and promotions to squeeze the most money out of each membership at our club.

But that goes against how *we* want to be treated as customers. We don't want to be constantly bombarded, so why would we want that for our members?

When people go into a gym, sometimes there are national and local businesses advertising within the club. Members know the club is making money by doing it. People understand why it's done, but it doesn't promote a stress-free, relaxing environment. It may cause people to start thinking about their work.

In addition to corporations, we were continually approached by people with small businesses or multilevel marketing companies who wanted to sell their wares at our club. While we appreciate small business owners and anyone working for themselves, we didn't want our members to feel like they were always being asked to buy something. So we turned down things like that.

The truth is, we all make enough decisions every day. People want their fitness club to be an oasis, somewhere to decompress as they exercise. We knew that and honored it. Yes, we could have made a few extra dollars by letting other companies hang banners on our walls, or having people in the welcome area demonstrating their products. But would it have been worth it, from a customer satisfaction standpoint? We felt it would not. Also, many of our members were business owners, and we knew they wouldn't want to see their competitor's brand staring them in the face at our club.

What we *did* focus on was being consistent with the member experience. We hired and retained excellent staff. We made sure equipment was up to date and functioning well. We kept everything spotlessly clean. We wanted our members to come in and think, *everything looks great and is working right. I can just enjoy my workout. I don't have to think about anything else for at least the next hour. I can count on Christi's to deliver.*

SUBLETTING SPACE

While we didn't have business advertising signs all over the place, there were a few services at our club that were not handled by us. In the new building, we created space for massage therapy and a Pilates studio. We charged a flat rent to massage therapists and Pilates instructors to use these spaces. They handled their own appointments and scheduling, but we were attentive, making sure they represented our brand well.

Flat rent was a deliberate choice. It allowed us to budget, knowing what we had coming in as a constant. For the massage therapists and Pilates instructors, it made business run more smoothly.

Many people doing that type of work come from situations where a percentage of what they earned was taken by the owner or the entity from which they rented space. Over time, they'd begin to resent this setup, because it meant the harder they worked, the more money the owners made.

These service providers stayed with us for years, and many continued with the new owners after we sold. Over the years, we raised their rent a little, but they made good money during their busy times. And when they were slow, they still paid us that guaranteed flat rent.

We always made sure any amenities we added complimented our business and fit into our vision statement.

REACHING OUT

When we attended the University of Florida in the mid-eighties, we heard about a health club that was thriving off campus even though the students had free access to modern health club facilities on the school grounds. Gainesville Health & Fitness, owned by Joe Cirulli, was successfully able to compete and build a culture of community at its club.

Their focus was recruiting and training the right people for their organization. They innovated in many ways, but the one that stood out was the assistance they provided on the weight room floor at all times. Their floor trainers were dressed in collared shirts and pants (and ties for the guys). These employees would be available to all members at no additional fee, to assist them in setting up equipment properly and to offer advice on form, weight settings and exercise frequency. This addressed one of the biggest barriers to success for a new exerciser: not knowing where to begin or how to use the equipment.

Gainesville Health & Fitness became one of the best health clubs in the nation and reached the goal of making Gainesville *"The Healthiest Community in America."* They have expanded to three locations in the county and have become esteemed leaders in the fitness industry.

Joe Cirulli is a well-known presenter and advocate for growing fitness leaders. I learned about his experience and success through fitness conferences and industry magazines. Even with his busy schedule he responded to my emails and calls asking for advice, and agreed to several meetings over the years we owned our club.

One meeting was just months before we were ready to break ground on our new 28,000-square foot facility. I heard physical therapy was a good profit center to have in a health club and many in our area were adding this service. Joe had an extensive background in operating a physical therapy business at his main location. He had benefited personally from the rehabilitation he received after an accident, and had a passion to provide the same service to others.

I started talking to him about our new facility and asked him what he thought about developing a space for physical therapy. He asked me, "Why do you want to include physical therapy in your new club?" I responded, "I've heard it's a good money maker." He said, "That's the worst reason to do it."

I was surprised at his response, but thought through what he said. I learned later how much I didn't know about that industry. Ultimately, it wouldn't have been a good fit for our club or culture.

He didn't tell me what I wanted to hear, but what I needed to hear. It was a valuable lesson about business and leadership.

I reached out to others in our industry and received good counsel on many occasions. Asking for advice from industry leaders was intimidating. It required humility and a willingness to admit you need help. But it connected us with great leaders and helped our whole organization.

THE COMPETITION

As mentioned in the previous chapter, there were new gyms popping up in our area every six months. We had Planet Fitness, Anytime Fitness, Curves, Relentless, Orangetheory, numerous yoga studios, barre studios, personal training, and small group training facilities, among others.

Looking back, we realize all that competition really made us dig deep and be introspective. We had to ask ourselves: **What is our core business, and what do we do better than everyone else?**

In *Good to Great*, Jim Collins talks about the "hedgehog concept." He explains that a hedgehog has a very good mechanism for self-defense. It rolls up in a ball, and its spines stick out all over. No other animal wants to mess with the hedgehog, because it's going to get poked.

The hedgehog doesn't need to continually figure out other ways to defend itself. It established this one thing, then proceeded to do it very, very well—better than anyone else.

In much the same manner, our two specialties were:

- **Structured children's programs, with a goal of having kids learn life lessons along with developing athletic ability.** Besides working on balance, coordination, strength, and flexibility, kids learned how to interact with their peers, respect authority, have compassion for others, and develop interpersonal skills. We knew we did this type of program well, better than anyone else in our community.

- **Adult group exercise, with a focus on innovative classes and high-quality instruction.** Our members created their daily routines around our classes. They were eager to try out new classes we brought in, because they knew we'd only bring in a new program if we could offer first-rate instruction for it. These things told us that we were offering people something they couldn't get anywhere else in town.

Our general manager was more concerned about the competition then he should have been. We urged him not to be reactive. We paid attention to the competition, but we used that information to help us define and identify who *we* should be, rather than attempt to mimic what everyone else was doing.

SELLING RIGHT

"Can I help you?"

We've all heard this when we walk into a business. Sounds friendly, but do they really want to help? Isn't the actual meaning, "I hope you buy something"?

It's rare to find a salesperson who actually wants to help you. Let's face it, most of the time salespeople are more bother than help. In many businesses, it's what they're trained and expected to do.

When we visited other health clubs, we often encountered troubling sales systems. One involved Steve having to go into "Sales Office B" to retrieve his driver's license, which was required for "security reasons" before they'd take him on a tour of the facility. Other visits involved "specials" that were good for *today*, and *today only!* These types of sales practices look at the customer as if they're a dollar bill, not a person.

We always thought our quality of service, environment, and culture should do the selling for us. This principle motivated us to constantly reinvest in the club, showing members and prospective members that we truly cared about their experience in our facility.

We decided the majority of our marketing dollars was better spent by investing *inside* the club than by paying for ads and promotions. Our job was to make the club the absolute best it could be. If we did that, sincere sales pitches came from our members directly to their friends and family.

In choosing between directing marketing dollars toward prospective members or existing members, we leaned towards investing internally, in ways that kept our current members happy. That meant things like buying new equipment, upgrading the flooring, painting the walls, and giving the staff raises.

In other words, we invested in the number one marketing and sales tool: word of mouth.

People love talking about their positive experiences. Your job as a business owner is to create memorable moments for your customers. Show them what a wonderful business looks and acts like.

It doesn't have to be complicated or expensive. For example, we trained our front-desk staff to give everyone who walked in the door a warm smile and a big hello. As people left, they received a friendly goodbye. It didn't matter if it was a member, a prospective member, a delivery person, or someone who wandered in off the street looking for directions to get somewhere else. Whoever walked in, they became the most important person in the room.

The idea is to sell the *right* things:

- Responsiveness to problems
- Willingness to go above and beyond to serve the customer
- Ability to learn people's names and get to know people personally
- Connection between staff and members

These "sales" do not translate directly into monetary transactions. But they differentiate you from the competition. They bring in more loyal, long-term customers. They make your business truly stand out.

THE COMPLEX WORLD OF MARKETING

Spending money on promo items—something customers can see, touch, and take home—is easy and fun. What business owner doesn't love seeing people using items with their business's logo on them?

But shelling out advertising dollars isn't quite as straightforward. Steve says, "When you buy print ads, radio ads, and online ads, the return on investment isn't always tangible or definitive. It's short lived, and you don't know if it makes a difference for the long run. You feel like you have to do it, but you're not sure if it will generate the results you're after."

We spent thousands of dollars on marketing, and to this day, we don't know which (if any) aspects paid off. Early on in running our club, there wasn't as much online advertising as there is today. Now that online advertising is abundant, marketing in general is a less costly proposition. If we were still running the business, we'd definitely lean toward online promotional opportunities. Not so much to *sell,* but to communicate the joy of our brand.

One thing we knew for sure: a bad review was very costly. Online reviews give customers leverage over businesses, and they're not afraid to use that leverage. As we mentioned earlier, direct confrontation is difficult for everyone, but writing a negative online review when they're fired up and angry is very, very easy for anybody to do.

We learned that it was marketing money well spent to refund a customer a meaningful sum of money *before* they wrote that bad review, rather than to try to address a bad review after the fact. Once that review is up, it's there to stay. Even if you respond online and apologize, you can't make the review itself go away. We maintained a 4.7 out of 5-star rating on various search engines and marketing sites, which was one of the keys to growing and selling our business.

The best marketing has always been, and will always be, working as hard as you can to provide the best customer experience possible, even when dealing with the most difficult customers.

Maybe it isn't so complex: ***Treat people the way you want to be treated.***

Words of wisdom from the world's best-selling book: The Bible.

LESSONS FROM A NEAR-TRAGEDY

As mentioned earlier, during the first couple of years running the business, we added spin classes. At that point, in the late 1990s, indoor cycling was a new concept that was showing success in some areas. But it wasn't yet offered in our area, and we wanted to get a jump on that.

We identified five strong candidates to get certified and brought in a presenter to train these instructors. The bikes were expensive, but they were specialized for the program. We leased twenty-six new cycles, hoping it would pay off. Bright lights and mirrors were the norm for group exercise at the time, and we used what we had.

Christi thought Steve would be a good fit as an instructor, because he's an outdoor cyclist—and he self-admits to having insufficient coordination to lead any other classes. So, Steve was one of the five instructors who were trained and began teaching spin classes.

"With spin," Steve explains, "I'd found my teaching niche. The buzz was building, and the classes were filling. I loved matching music to the drills, to deliver a colorful, challenging workout."

But then, just as things were taking off, a phone call brought Steve to his knees. After taking Steve's class, a participant suffered a heart attack behind the wheel of his car. His wife managed to grab the steering wheel, reach the brake pedal, and keep them from crashing. The man was airlifted to a hospital in Orlando.

Steve remembers thinking, *I might have killed a man. I should never have been pushing the class that hard. I'm not qualified to do this. I need to quit.*

To this day, Steve says, "I have never felt so responsible for someone else's life as I did when I got that phone call."

To our relief, the next day we were told that the man had survived and was stable. Steve was immensely grateful, but he still felt he should quit teaching spin, to ensure it never happened again.

As we got more information, we learned that our cyclist had a blockage that was brought on by the spin class exertion. That made sense, but what we *didn't* know before this event was that the man was a pilot. The doctors told him to be thankful his heart attack had happened when it did—not at 20,000 feet. They said it was inevitable that it would happen, and it was a blessing it turned out to be a manageable situation.

Steve says, "I learned two vital lessons from that experience. One, you shouldn't jump to conclusions, because you can't see God's plan until He reveals it. And two, don't quit. Don't let fear do the talking."

ASK THE MEMBERS

Some of the best changes we made were based on suggestions from members. People will not hesitate to give their opinion and suggestions. Whenever we implemented a member-generated or staff-generated idea, it strengthened the organization and brought diversity to the club.

For example, that spin program mentioned above? Due to the program's success, we expanded, creating a dedicated spin room.

Our accountant took spin classes and mentioned that it might be a good idea to dim the lights and get rid of the mirrors.

Another lesson learned. They kept coming when we opened our hearts and minds.

LOOKING OUT THE WINDOW

Gyms are notorious for what we'd call "looking in the mirror"—in other words, only looking inside our own industry for inspiration. Many gyms borrow most of their ideas from other gyms. This "in the mirror" line of thinking kept our industry in a holding pattern for years.

Eventually, some health clubs started looking at other industries for inspiration. We'd call those club owners the "look out the window" types of business owners. Such club owners realized that there was much to learn from the hotel, restaurant, and entertainment fields.

Steve read a book describing this trend and decided to look at successful companies outside of fitness for ideas. The three he ended up focusing on were Disney, Starbucks, and Apple.

- **Disney** is close to home (in Orlando). As Floridians, we've always marveled at how they make you feel like you're in a different world. The cleanliness at Walt Disney World is immediately apparent. Everything is immaculate, and the staff is happily roaming the park cleaning. Considering this, we decided that in our club, cleanliness would always be a high priority. We also made sure our interior featured bright lighting, outdoor themes, and unique finishes. We also installed speakers outside the building so you would start experiencing our brand even before you entered the club. Disney had music playing throughout the park to lift your mood and enhance your experience even before you got on a ride.

- **Starbucks** had Steve's attention because of the consistency of their products, even as they constantly expand their locations and offerings. Everywhere Starbucks does business, people leave their cafés with a pep in their step. Our goal for the club was for members to do the same after a workout (minus the caffeine). How could we model Starbucks' success in our gym? We decided it was by ensuring that everything was always operational, and staff was ready with smiles and great attitudes. We also constantly evaluated our offerings and added new classes with the same quality instruction as our existing classes.

- **Apple** has always set the bar for changing the way people look at the future. They've shown individuals and companies that anything is possible. In the same way, at Christi's, we wanted members to sense that we were always looking ahead and brought innovation regularly to our customers.

CREATING "DIFFERENT"

We love different, and when we owned the club, we loved to create it. Over the years, members often remarked that there was something different about our place. They'd say the "feel" was uplifting.

We give God all the glory for those statements. When we are in our area of gifting, He encourages our hearts. How do we know if it's God or just our thoughts? Our belief is that if it involves genuinely serving others, it's likely God leading us. We believe that He provides the ultimate experience, if we're willing to follow.

Case in point: as mentioned in the previous chapter, behind the welcome desk in our new facility, there was a thirty-foot-wide by ten-foot-high curved radius wall. When we first opened, this wall was blank, but it was just begging for something to be displayed on it.

Steve says, "I saw the beach in my head and knew we had to cover that wall with God's creation: the sky, the ocean, and the shore. Nature is beautiful and enduring, and our club was in a coastal town. What could be more perfect?"

Great! But how?

Steve researched large format printing and found a place in Delray Beach, Florida that provided this service. He bought several high-resolution photos of beach scenes and headed south to see what was possible.

Steve says, "When I walked in the door of this company, there was an amazing beach scene behind their front desk! The picture was far better than what I'd found, and I wished I could get that photo. I asked if that was possible, and they were happy to give me the digital photo at no charge if I printed with them. I ended up finding other photos I liked on their walls, too. When I asked the printer if I could get them on single pieces of vinyl at the large sizes I needed, he asked me to follow him to the back of the warehouse. I'll never forget it. They were working on printing Shaquille O'Neal ninety feet tall and thirty feet wide, to hang on the outside of the American Airlines Arena in Miami! God definitely led me to the right place. I knew these wall coverings were going to be a special addition to the culture and look of our club."

Steve ordered four vinyl wallscapes: one for behind the welcome desk, the second for the spin room, the third for the weight room, and the fourth for the group exercise studio. This was in 2004, when this type of printing on vinyl was uncommon in rural areas like ours. But the printing technology was improving, and we were able to get beautiful, high-resolution images on our walls for less than two dollars per square foot.

Different, here we come!

———

"Whatever you do, be different—that was the advice my mother gave me, and I can't think of better advice for an entrepreneur. If you're different, you will stand out."
– Anita Roddick

———

WHAT'S OUR MESSAGE?

At one point, our slogan (and mission statement) was "We Make Fitness Fun." By providing great programming, introducing innovations in fitness, and refusing to settle for average—all the while delivering our services in a bright, uplifting environment—we encouraged members to find working out fun and rewarding.

Our goal was to develop a culture where members felt like they belonged. We wanted our members to look at their lives in a different light. We wanted them to see all the possibilities that being healthy brings.

ELEVATE THE ORDINARY

- What methods can you use to keep up with trends in your industry? When you're caught up in the day-to-day operations of running a business, you can miss out on the trends of tomorrow. It takes organization and planning to stay on top of what's coming next.

- Are you overthinking who your competition is? Remember that it's more important to define who *you* are and what you're trying to achieve.

- While you don't want to be reactive to the competition, it's important to understand their pricing, services, and target markets. Use this information to carve out your section of the market, rather than trying to overlap your market with theirs.

- Does your quality of service do your sales for you? If not, in what ways can you reinvest to show customers you care about them, both before and after the sale?

- Are you using the most effective marketing tool there is: word of mouth? How can you enhance customer service to ensure people are recommending your business to others?

- Are you "looking in the mirror" or "looking out the window"? Which corporations or businesses inspire you, even those in industries other than your own?

CHAPTER SEVEN

EXPECTING THE UNEXPECTED

NAVIGATING THROUGH THE CHALLENGES OF BUSINESS

In the twenty-one years we owned our club, we experienced some incredible highs, and a few heartbreaking lows. Because we feel it's important to be realistic, in this chapter we'll talk about both.

Sometimes, when there's good news and bad news, we want to hear the bad news first, to get it out of the way. In that spirit, we'll discuss life in the valleys before moving on to the mountaintops.

GETTING INTO DEBT

By our third year in business, we'd expanded, which was great for staff and member morale, not to mention *our* morale. Steve says, "I remember driving home from the club one night and feeling like I'd used almost every gift or ability that I had that day—but instead of being exhausted, I felt fulfilled. And it had nothing to do with money, because we were very much in the red."

The truth is, at that point we were still losing money. Our excitement about what we were achieving was high, but the balance in our bank account was low.

Or, to put it more accurately, our credit card balances were much too high. We'd begun taking out extra credit cards to fund the business, because the local bank decided our numbers didn't look good enough for additional loans. As mentioned earlier, they wanted us to pay back our current loans before borrowing more. We'd gotten to the point where our credit card debt was $200,000.

We knew that paying the interest on one credit card with another card was not a good financial plan for our club. This caused us to face the dismal truth that we might not be able to stay in business.

Prior to opening the club, we'd heard that being undercapitalized is one of the biggest mistakes new business owners make. But when you're a new entrepreneur, you think you're going to be different. There's a book called *The E Myth*, by Michael E. Gerber, that talks about this. Gerber says this is a very common thought process of an entrepreneur: *Yes, I know fifty percent of businesses fold within the first two years. But that's not going to be me.*

It's a bit of a blind spot. And we'd fallen into it.

But now, we figured it was the end of our journey. With sadness and resignation, Steve made an appointment with a bankruptcy lawyer. When they sat down to meet, Steve explained our situation to the lawyer.

The lawyer's response was, "Oh, those banks got you into this trouble. Those greedy banks allowed you to borrow all this money." He handed Steve a bankruptcy application. "We can get you out from under all this. They shouldn't have loaned you that money. They shouldn't have approved you for the cards."

Wait. Was it really the bank's fault, or the credit card companies' fault? Something inside of Steve said that wasn't right. He didn't fill out the application. He told the lawyer we'd think about it and get back to him.

Following the appointment, Steve sat in his car, mulling it over. He explains, "Despite what that lawyer said, I didn't feel the banks did anything wrong. *I* was the one who borrowed the money. *I* was the one who signed the applications for the credit cards."

He goes on, "I remember having a conversation with God, sitting in my car. I said, 'God, I know that in Your Word, it says we're to pay back what we owe. Please, help me find a way to repay this debt."

God provides wisdom when we reach out to Him. But He also expects us to be proactive. Steve didn't assume God would "solve the problem" for us. But asking for His help did point us toward good people who sent us in the right direction. To us, it's about the asking. It's about a willingness to do the right thing. We believe that if we're willing to take responsibility for our actions and not blame someone else, God honors that.

Our faith has and continues to help us tremendously, both in business and in life.

DEBT CONSOLIDATION AND STEVE'S SECOND JOB

Two things happened: credit card debt consolidation and a second job for Steve.

After the appointment with the bankruptcy lawyer, Steve went home and researched credit counseling services. The one we chose advised us to immediately dissolve all the credit cards except a single card that we kept open for business expenses. That was step one. Then we consolidated all the outstanding debt into a single debt with a monthly payment.

Credit consolidation carried a temporary mark on our credit report, but we were committed to repaying our obligations, and this was the fastest route. The service helped us lay out a five-year plan to clear out all the credit card debt. Five years at $3,000 a month definitely hurt. But the interest rate on our repayment was 6%, and a conventional bank loan was generally 9%—*if* we'd been able to get a conventional bank loan, which we were not.

We were committed to finding a way to pay the $3,000 a month, pay it on time, and pay it in full. Again, we believe God came through: two weeks after the moment in the parking lot, Steve received a phone call, asking if he wanted a job at the tennis club down the road.

This particular business, a tennis and fitness club, was under new ownership, and they were looking for a manager. Being known in Vero Beach tennis circles, Steve's name was brought up. They offered him $40,000 a year. He'd work days at the tennis club and nights at Christi's. It might even be sort of fun, Steve thought.

That notion was short lived. His first day on the job, Steve received a fax from the new owners saying their fitness center was losing money and would need to be shut down eventually. Nice first day! Steve says, "I could anticipate the gossip. 'Did you hear that the owner of the health club two miles north is shutting down the club he's the manager for?'"

As it turned out, that club was able to limp along for a while. In all honesty, the tennis part of their business wasn't a winner, either, and eighteen months after Steve took the job, the money stopped coming in to pay the bills. That was Steve's signal that it was time to devote all his efforts to Christi's again.

But Steve's two-job stint for eighteen months went a long way toward paying down our debt, and by then, business was picking up at Christi's. By year four, we were breaking even. In year five, we started to generate a profit.

Five years later, year eight of running Christi's Fitness, we had a zero balance on the single credit card we still had open. Just as importantly, we had a covenant with each other (and with God) to pay the balance on that card in full, every month.

End of story. (Because in retrospect, this *was* almost the end of our story.)

HINDSIGHT IS 20/20

In year three, when we expanded our space, we took a calculated risk. We thought it would pay off sooner than it did. Eventually, it *did* pay off, in increased memberships, but it took longer than we'd anticipated.

But in all that time—except for the dark moment when we considered bankruptcy—we continued to believe in ourselves, our business, and God. We had confidence that somehow, we'd make it work.

Successful entrepreneurs generally feel this way. They have confidence that they'll figure it out. They persevere. They have passion and a driving belief that their business is worthwhile. And they'll do anything to keep it afloat.

Confidence and perseverance are admirable qualities. That being said, how you'll finance your business is something you *must* consider, long before opening your doors.

In the end, things worked out for us, but it was stressful, exhausting, and almost broke us. We share this story as a cautionary tale.

At the same time, in our experience and that of many other successful entrepreneurs, everyone from Walt Disney to Steve Jobs, it's not unusual to borrow more money than initially planned for, from banks, credit cards, family, or investors. It's something to think carefully about as you start and grow your business.

———

"I always did something I was a little not ready to do. I think that's how you grow. When there's that moment of 'Wow, I'm not really sure I can do this,' and you push through those moments, that's when you have a breakthrough."
– Marissa Mayer

———

LEARNING OUR LESSONS

In many ways, we were fortunate that our near-bankruptcy experience happened somewhat early in running our business. From that day on, we paid our credit card balance in full, every month. We never carried a balance after that.

The only other time we incurred substantial debt was when we were getting a construction loan for our new, expanded facility. In the next chapter, we'll discuss specifics about our expansion journey. Here, let's examine how we paid off our debt for it.

We were able to take out a Small Business Administration loan for building the new space. By that time, our club was showing a profit, and the bank could see how we'd conscientiously paid off our credit card debt. When we brought our expansion plans to the bank and applied for a loan, we were a much more appealing customer than a few years earlier, when we asked for a loan simply to keep the business afloat.

To pay off the building debt quickly and aggressively, we took advantage of the fact that business was booming. We went from 13,000 square feet to 28,000 square feet, and memberships increased right along with the expanded space. When we got into the new building, we were at about $750,000 a year in gross revenue. In 2004, the first full year in the new building, our gross revenue was around $900,000. And the numbers kept getting better. We went to $1.1 million, then $1.2 million. By 2007, we were at $1.5 million in gross revenue. Our profit margin was 10% to 15%. We were even paying ourselves good salaries.

This happened right before the 2008 recession. Because we'd paid off our original debt and were conscientiously and consistently paying off the building debt, the recession hit us, but it didn't break us. If we'd still had our original debt *and* had been paying the minimum on the building debt when the recession hit, there's no way we would have been able to continue running the business.

WEATHERING THE RECESSION

When the recession hit, many fitness clubs reduced their prices. We started seeing other privately-owned clubs offer $19.99-a-month memberships, in an effort to compete with Planet Fitness and others charging only $10 a month.

We didn't do that. We held our prices steady. And actually, our industry supported that position. They said we shouldn't try to compete with the low-cost clubs. Our goal was to be the premium fitness club in our area, and the recession did not change that goal. In a high-end business like ours, the overhead structure is so much different than in a large, corporately owned low-cost club. If we'd tried to compete with them, we knew we'd do ourselves and our members a major disservice, and maybe go out of business.

It was actually our kids' programs that kept us afloat. Many of our long-term adult members stayed with us; this type of member was committed to the club, no matter what. But there were also many members for whom the main draw was our children's programs. We found that when such people are looking to pinch pennies, they'll take away their own thing—but not their kid's thing. They'll think, *okay, I don't need to take classes at the gym. Maybe I can walk outside while my child is in gymnastics class.* If a child is begging to do an activity they love, parents will sacrifice their own activity before they'll sacrifice the child's activity.

Our market focus was middle to high income earners, especially once we were in the new facility. We wanted to attract and retain members who appreciated a quality facility with quality programming, and were willing and able to pay for it. The recession did not change our approach. Nonetheless, we needed to address the reality that for some of our members, their financial picture was less secure than it had been in the pre-recession days.

Our response to the recession was to let members go month-to-month for the same monthly rate as a year-long commitment. During that time, we didn't require that members sign a year-long agreement. We said to them, "We know things are uncertain. We want you to feel comfortable. We don't want you to feel like you're locked into anything."

Another thing we did during the recession was to take a good, hard look at our staffing. Who wasn't performing at the highest level? Who was not being as productive as they could be?

We had to make some tough decisions. Layoffs are never fun, but we had to consolidate our staff. It was very difficult, but we knew it was necessary in order to stay in business. Steve assumed many of those staff members' duties. That was what it took to make it through.

What did we learn from this? One thing that came out of it was that evaluating staff was something we needed to do regularly. We had to be willing to speak directly with staff and give them a chance to improve. But if they were dragging their feet or their attitude wasn't right, they needed to be removed. This was true even if they'd been with us a long time. Long-term employment doesn't mean people should be given a free pass to stay on indefinitely.

That was a tough lesson to learn and to implement. But after the recession, we realized it was a healthy pruning that took place. We also decided we'd continue to offer a month-to-month option for membership. We wanted the club experience to retain members, not a contract.

LAWSUITS

In our twenty-one years in business, we were only successfully sued twice. In our industry, that's a low number. Christi says, "There's a woman who runs a large gymnastics center in Indiana. She's one of the premier gymnastics people in the United States, and she speaks all over the country. One time, I was sitting in a lecture she was giving. She'd been in business for twenty years. She said her club had only been sued thirteen times. Hearing that, I felt pretty good about our number."

In our industry, a successful lawsuit generally involves the insurance company having to pay out after someone is injured. In the world of fitness, there are inherent risks. Gymnasts get sprains or a broken bone. We had people faint in the gym. We had people who, as they fainted, fell into a piece of equipment and were injured.

Our insurance company advised us that if our members felt a loyalty to us, they'd be less likely to sue if something happened to them or their child at our gym. Knowing this, we followed up when something happened. Say a child broke a bone in the gymnastics room. It was no one's fault; it was just an accident. Steve would make an immediate, same-day call to the parent. He'd follow through to check on the child. If the family didn't have insurance, we'd cover an X-ray, CT scan, or whatever was needed. This was less costly for us than reporting it to our insurance company— and much less costly than a lawsuit. In most cases, the member was satisfied that we'd done all we could.

You might wonder if we had waivers, and if so, weren't they enough? After all, if someone signed a waiver and then got hurt at our gym, that was *their* problem, right?

This is true in theory, but a lot of waivers don't hold up in court. That's not a reason to skip having them. Before engaging in an activity, people should be aware of the risks. But if it came to a day in court, we knew a plaintiff's lawyer would do everything they could to pick apart our waiver.

We saw no reason to run that risk. We always tried to resolve the situation ourselves, long before it came to that. Sometimes that meant paying a deductible or paying medical bills. It might mean paying for treatments for someone who was injured. Or psychotherapy sessions for a kid who got lost looking for the restroom. He went in the men's locker room and didn't know where he was, and he needed five hours of therapy to work through it. Five hours of a therapist's time cost us a lot less than a lawsuit.

Most of the time, people realized we were trying to do the right thing. We only had a few unreasonable people. We had two that sued us successfully. The first one happened in the gymnastics room. A little girl did a cartwheel and landed badly. We found out later, through the child's grandparents, that she broke her arm and that her father was very upset he didn't hear from us.

This incident slipped through the cracks. Staff did not make us aware of it, so Steve never made a phone call. The staff had assumed it was a minor sprain. They sent the child home, thinking it was no big deal. They didn't follow through with us, which ended up being very costly. The result was a lawsuit, with a payout.

Afterward, we made sure to emphasize to all staff that if anything happened, no matter how small, we needed to know about it right away.

The second successful lawsuit was an incident where a grandmother was in the room during a Mommy and Me class. She fell on the trampoline. Immediately after she fell, she turned to her daughter and said, "Go get my phone." She took pictures of her skinned knee and where she fell.

Right away, we knew we were in trouble with that one. We found out later that she'd had other payouts. Steve was at the gym that day, and he attempted to talk with her about the incident, but she wouldn't speak with him. He tried to get her to go to a doctor, but she refused. She was focused on making sure her pictures were taken. She was a serial lawsuit person. It wouldn't have mattered where it happened or how it was handled. She was intent on suing, and she won.

A third incident almost happened: A member fell off a spin bike. Afterward, we paid for massage and acupuncture. At one point, Steve realized we'd spent a couple thousand dollars on these treatments, and the member kept coming back to us for more. Steve told him we couldn't pay for further treatments.

The member said, "Then I'm going to sue you over it."

"But you only fell off a bike," Steve replied. "You've had a lot of treatment. You should be fine now."

The guy said, "I've got testicular cancer as a result of the fall. I'm going to sue you."

"I don't think you can get cancer from falling off a bike," Steve said.

The guy insisted he did. It was clear that this individual was just after our money.

Steve called our insurance company and said, "I think I've really messed up here." He explained the situation, then said, "I feel that by continuing to give him money, I've admitted some guilt, some culpability."

Our insurance agent explained that in Florida, there's something called the Good Samaritan Act. According to this law, if the guy took us to court to sue, we could bring up our previous attempts to make good on the situation, and it would likely be looked at favorably. In the end, the member decided not to sue.

We were lucky with that one. Florida is the most sue-friendly state in the country. There are more personal injury attorneys per square mile in Florida than in any other state.

Honestly, when the timing was right for selling the business, that was a point in favor of doing so. By then, we'd become tired of having to worry about things like this.

PROGRAMS THAT DIDN'T TAKE OFF

Sometimes, we'd try a program and it wouldn't work. For instance, we attempted a couple of times to have programs for teens, and we never really hit it off with that. We'd hoped to target a teen market that was not already exercising or playing a sport. We implemented a "get off the couch" type of program for teens. Although parents would have loved it if their kids embraced such a program, the teens themselves were not as enthused. A parent would drive their teen to the gym for a program like that, and the teen would grudgingly do it, but they were never really into it.

We always had teen athletes who trained at the gym. These kids were on the other end of the fitness spectrum. These were the kids whose parents hired one of our club's trainers for their star athlete, someone to help their teen take their sport to the next level. But that type of teen didn't need a "get off the couch program," and, unfortunately, for the kids who needed them, such programs were not popular.

The weight management program was another challenge. When we first opened the business, our weight management program was very successful. We had forty or fifty people, and the average weight loss over the twelve-week program was about 8.7 pounds. But, as mentioned earlier, we sensed that most people were too intimidated to talk about weight loss in a health club. We realized that a specific weight loss program was not going to work as well as we'd thought. We'd thought it would be a natural fit, but that turned out to be untrue. So, we dropped the program.

In both instances, we realized in a timely fashion that these programs were not a good fit for us, but they weren't going to drive us out of business. We just had to change our approach. In the case of the weight loss program, we made a major change by dropping both the program and the mention of it from our name. Fortunately, we realized this early on, so it didn't negatively affect our branding.

GETTING THE RATS OUT

In college, Steve was the manager of a male rooming house. He was responsible for collecting rent, keeping the peace, and making sure the place was clean. It was mostly graduate students getting cheap rent in a very old, two-story house with twelve rooms. It had two shared bathrooms and one kitchen. Steve tried to get the residents to keep the kitchen in reasonable shape, but it was a challenge. The building probably wouldn't have passed code, if it had ever been inspected. If the inspectors looked at it after a football weekend, it might have been condemned.

Steve was responsible for cleaning the bathrooms. He says, "When I took the job, it didn't sound too bad, especially because I was living there rent-free. But once I started actually doing it, I was surprised how bad it could get. I'd hold my breath as I cleaned up vomit, feces, urine, and hair from the showers and toilet areas. I remember thinking, *this is why I'm getting my college degree—so I don't have to spend my entire life doing jobs like this.* It probably was a factor in motivating me to keep up my classwork and graduate."

Steve also thought, *this is the most disgusting thing I will ever have to do in my life.* And he was right about that for many years, until he was trying to figure out why there was a terribly bad odor in the gym, getting stronger each day. It took him a couple of days to determine it was coming from the ceiling. He set up a ladder and took out one of the ceiling tiles to look around up there. It was so dark, he couldn't see, but he could sense he was getting close to the source.

Steve grabbed a flashlight, put his head through the hole, and started panning the light in a circle. He couldn't understand how the smell could be so bad when he couldn't see anything amiss. He was almost done with his 360-degree inspection when he came face to face with an eight-inch-long, dead rat.

Steve says, "I don't think I used any of the ladder steps on the way back down."

The rat had likely come from the restaurant in our same building, just another unwanted surprise of business ownership. Steve could have called the pest control service to come and remove it, but he had finally discovered the source of the lingering smell and he wanted it out *now*.

Steve thought, *how bad could it be? After all, I've cleaned up after a football weekend.*

With what turned out to be overconfidence, he went back up the ladder, carrying a plastic bag and a dustpan. Then the reality of what he was attempting hit him. He squinted his eyes to blur his vision, so he wouldn't have to look into the dead rat's open eyes as he attempted to scoop it into the bag.

He says, "I was ultimately successful, but I realized the event trumped bathroom cleanup at the rooming house. I had nightmares afterward. Worse, it wouldn't be the last rat I had to remove. But that's the price of being in business for yourself."

TO CATCH A THIEF

Sometime around 2008, we noticed that protein bars were disappearing off a counter-height rack in our pro shop. It was close to where some mischievous kids liked to sit, supposedly doing their homework. It's got to be those kids, we decided. They're probably stealing the bars.

We counted the bars. We put up a camera, focused directly on the rack of protein bars. We looked at the tapes daily. Nothing.

Then we fast-forwarded through, and all of a sudden, we saw something on the tape late at night. We rewound and watched again. A rat scaled up vertically, right to the top, grabbed a bar in its mouth, and pulled it underneath the furniture. Then it went back, got another one, and pulled it underneath.

Looking under the furniture, we found wrappers and half-eaten bars. And that rat was getting pumped up! It was eating all this protein—and, most likely, procreating.

Nobody wants the fittest rat to survive. We had a service bait the entire inside and outside of the facility to get the rat, its babies, and all its friends out.

It was a hassle, but it was also kind of funny. We thought somebody was stealing, and they were! Just not the somebody we thought it was.

ANOTHER KIND OF RAT

We also had a different kind of rat infiltrate, in the form of a male gymnastics coach. Male coaches were in high demand, as it's generally easier for men than women to spot an older tumbler or gymnast. Often, a male coach can help kids feel more confident practicing higher-level skills.

We always wanted to see the best in people, and when a middle-aged coach applied for a job, we gave him a shot. His references checked out, and we were looking forward to bringing his gymnastics experience to our program. But soon, his true personality came out, and we needed to let him go.

He decided it would be a good idea to take all the student rosters as he left the building, likely in hopes of contacting them at his next job and potentially poaching them for other clubs.

We knew a police officer from the club, and the officer paid him an unofficial visit, to rattle his cage. When you make a little noise, rats scatter. We're pretty sure this "rat" didn't contact any of our gymnasts.

FOCUSING ON THE POSITIVE

The unexpected negatives were mostly out of our control and difficult to avoid. But as an entrepreneur, what is in your control is creating a positive culture in the midst of all the unknowns.

LEARNING TO ACCEPT ACCOUNTABILITY

We like Merriam-Webster's definition of accountability: "An obligation or willingness to accept responsibility or to account for one's actions." If everyone lived by this principle, it might solve most of the world's problems.

As a business owner, if you hold yourself accountable, it will benefit your business in the long run. Justification can poison your business and your life. You might not even know you're drinking it, because it tastes good going down.

In our experience, there's only one way to know if justification will kill you: tell someone else about it. Let them taste it, and see how *they* react.

Steve says, "There was a group of three men I met with regularly to discuss the tough stuff. One time during the years when we were taking out new credit cards to pay the balances on our existing cards, I told them what I was doing. They called me on it and said it would kill my business. I made a commitment to them that I would make it right, and they made a commitment that they would ask me about it again. When I had that moment in my car, talking to God about not filing for bankruptcy but instead taking responsibility for my actions, I thought about these three friends. I was going to have to tell them how I planned to solve the problem. Did I really want to say that I was declaring bankruptcy, that I was trying to make my problems disappear without holding myself accountable? Like having a relationship with God, having these men in my life was a reminder that accountability isn't a one-time event. It has to be ongoing to make a difference in your life."

Steve goes on, "What could have been a complete negative actually turned into a positive. I don't feel good about how we got into that situation—but even now, all these years later, I feel very good about how we got out of it."

SERVING CHILDREN IN OUR COMMUNITY

Children are good for the business of life. They are amazing gifts. Whether ours or someone else's, children teach us some of life's greatest lessons. The wonder they show when taking in the simplest aspects of God's creations is an example to us all. The innocence and vulnerability they display is what's often lacking in our lives as we get older.

Throughout our years in business, we served thousands of children. Gymnastics, dance, swimming, and martial arts were the main children's programs we offered. We also ran a Speed Academy and summer camps, and we hosted birthday parties.

Our gymnastics programs were very popular, and thus had an impact on the highest number of children we served. It's easy to see why gymnastics is a foundation for any sport. But, as mentioned earlier, it also teaches great life lessons. Being parents ourselves, we could appreciate the long-term value in our gymnastics programs. Learning to respect authority, having patience, setting goals, practicing hard, encouraging others, being compassionate, and learning how to win and lose were just some of the lessons kids learned. In our view (and in the view of our gymnastics students' parents), those lessons are inherently more important than acquiring physical skills.

That being said, seeing a kid land their first cartwheel is awesome. Their eyes light up like they just won a million dollars.

Watching the community children become active at an early age, knowing it helped form good habits for life, was a rewarding part of our business. Many of these kids would go on to utilize our adult fitness programs, and, when they had kids of their own, would bring them to our children's programs. And some, like Shelley's daughter, Amanda, worked for us as they got older, establishing their first job experience.

If you're fortunate enough to have children of your own, the blessings increase exponentially. Blessings aren't always pleasant, though! But difficulties and trials raising children can yield hidden treasures, and the greatest of these is unconditional love. It's hard to understand, on a human level, how we manage to grow our love for a person even when some of that person's actions don't feel deserving of it. Both of us can remember being brought to the end of our patience levels, wondering how we would make it through the day, only to sense a deeper love for our children as we watched them sleep that night.

As a parent, every day you are faced with sacrifice and unselfishness. Even on the days we didn't feel like we made any progress with our children (or anything else), we knew God honored our effort. It demonstrated His unconditional love.

In our view, training children is much like faith. At times, things feel stagnant, and it's hard to sense any momentum. You feel like you're doing the same things over and over, and nothing is changing. But—as a gymnastics coach, a parent, or a person of faith—you know in your core that growth *is* happening, even when you can't see it. You trust and persevere. Having children forces us to do this, in the same way keeping faith during dark times yields great benefits in the long run.

EMPLOYEES WHO WENT ON TO BECOME ENTREPRENEURS

In earlier chapters, you met Don and Shelley. Reading on, you'll meet one more employee, Rachel, and another member, Laura.

All of the four people featured in this book are business owners. When we decided to share others' experiences with Christi's Fitness in this book, we didn't intentionally seek out fellow entrepreneurs. At the same time, it's no accident that we asked these particular people to share their stories. All of them are visionaries and, in one way or another, like-minded to us. We feel a kinship with each of them.

Over the years, eight former staff members went on to open their own fitness businesses. Five of them opened adult fitness facilities, including one small yoga studio and a couple of studios that focused on personal training. Three opened facilities specializing in structured kids' fitness programs.

Steve recalls when an employee came to him and said, "I want to be able to pay myself what I want to pay myself. I want to take vacations when I want to take vacations. That's why I want to own my own business."

Steve replied, "We wish you well. You'll get to learn a lot."

Rachel, whom you'll meet in the next chapter, owns a veterinary practice with her husband, who is a vet. But she also taught Pilates within our facility. We rented her space and promoted her services within the facility.

When an employee left to start their own business, we weren't always thrilled, but we knew that's what we'd done. Christi worked for other fitness facilities before we opened our club. There were a lot of people in the community who appreciated Christi's teaching skills. She knew that when we opened our own place, her former employer would lose some customers, as those customers gravitated toward us.

What's good for the goose is good for the gander, right? So, if we lost members when some of our former staff opened their own gyms, all we could say was, "You know what? They've developed themselves into confident leaders. They did that while working for us. We understand why some members might want to follow them to their new gyms. And we wish them well."

WORKING WITH CHARITIES

At a fitness conference, the topic of working with charities came up. The advice given was, "If it's a charity you believe in, always say yes when you're asked. You don't always have to give out money. You can provide a service."

We were compelled to be part of our community. When a charitable organization that aligned with our values asked us for a donation, we did it, no problem.

There's a women's refuge center in our community. It's a place for women coming from abusive or otherwise difficult situations.

They used to have a fundraiser where women would donate purses, and they'd sell the purses to raise money for the center. Numerous times, we provided a venue for that event. They'd use one of our studios, and quite a few of our members donated purses and attended the event. They'd do a big blast to promote it in the community, and we always promoted it within the facility, too.

Another local charity is called Hibiscus House. It's a place for children who are removed from situations of abuse or neglect. Hibiscus House provides a safe home and counseling for these children until a more permanent situation can be found. Every year at Christmas, we'd have a tree for them in our main area. Hibiscus House brought us tags for specific items that their resident kids wanted. Our members could take a couple of tags and buy the gifts.

At one point, Hibiscus House received grant money to try to do an internship-partnered program with businesses in our community. This was designed for older teens living at Hibiscus House. We took part in that. It wasn't as successful as they'd hoped it would be, but we were glad to help them give it a try.

In our Mommy and Me classes, we did "Bring a Friend Day." Mom and child invited friends to join in for the day. To take part in this special day, everyone had to bring a canned item. We donated the items to a food pantry.

We did St. Jude's fitness class fundraisers. We'd team-teach them, with multiple instructors and various themes. All the money raised was donated to St. Jude Children's Research Hospital.

For our spin class participants, we did American Cancer Society rides and classes. This was another worthwhile cause for which we were happy to raise money, and have a great time doing it.

When it came to charity asks, we didn't say yes 100% of the time. Over the years, we were approached by a few organizations that we found were not in alignment with us. That happened very infrequently—but if something felt off, we politely declined.

FUNDRAISERS AND COMMUNITY EVENTS

There were a few instances where a specific member had a problem, such as an unexpected illness or family crisis. We held fundraising classes for such members whenever we could.

We were always involved with the Christmas parades in town. Kids in our programs would build a float. The kids and coaches would walk with the float each year.

Our competitive team gymnasts hosted 5K races. This was to raise funds for their travel to meets.

We also hosted dance recitals. We started small. The recital was originally in our facility, just for the parents. Then we went to a bigger venue in town, a place called The Heritage Center with about a hundred seats. Eventually, we had as many as nine hundred people come to these recitals. When we got to that level, we'd rent the performing arts center at our local high school.

Our community meant a lot to us, still does, in fact. We knew we owed a certain amount of our success to being part of such a wonderful community, and we wanted to give back whenever we could.

SCHOLARSHIPS

We had a scholarship program in the club. If someone was in need, there was an application form they could fill out. It could be for an adult membership or a children's program. For example, a parent who wanted their child in gymnastics but couldn't afford it might apply for a scholarship.

We did many more scholarships on the kids' side than we did for adults About 85% of our scholarships were for kids' classes.

When we started the scholarship program, we donated the whole fee, but we quickly realized that was not a successful way to do it. When people paid a little something, they were more inclined to feel like it had value. So we asked them for a small contribution, even if it was as little as ten dollars a month.

Sometimes, we'd get a cancellation form from a long-term member, and their reason for leaving was something like, "I feel so sad about leaving, but I've lost my job. I'm going to have to put my membership on hold. But as soon as I can get back, I'm going to come back." In that case, we might call that member and offer them a couple of free months to get them through that tough time.

Whenever we were in a position to do this sort of thing, we did it. Again, this was a way to recognize our place in and gratitude for our community.

INTERNS

Christi ran our internship program. Most of the interns had an Exercise Physiology background. They were usually young people who wanted a path to stretch their skills. These were full-time positions for a set period of time, and the interns were given stipends.

They were excited to be doing, for example, body fat testing. They had practiced this skill in school, so it was good for them to get hands-on experience testing and explaining it to our members.

Having them in the facility was also good for the members, who enjoyed working with our interns and getting to know them.

Over the time she ran the intern program, Christi had four interns. We also had a fifth intern who worked directly with Don.

The interns would be given specific projects, based on their college expertise and their background. They were not just workhorses assigned to do "grunt" jobs. Their time needed to be planned, and their work had to have value.

For example, one of them was given the assignment of putting together an in-house triathlon. People would swim a certain number of laps in our pool, then go into the spin room and do a certain number of miles on the bike, then get on a treadmill and walk or run a certain number of miles.

The intern met in advance with every member who signed up. He did an evaluation of their fitness level, then gave them a training program. The goal was that in sixty days, they'd be ready for triathlon day. It was the intern's responsibility to meet with them regularly, encourage them, and keep them involved.

About fifty people signed up. We had triathletes who wanted to do it and who needed very little supervision or encouragement. But we also had people who had never done anything like that before, and they benefited from close interaction with our intern.

We held the triathlon on a Saturday morning. We ran it in heats of ten people. It was a lot of fun for members. Our first-time triathletes said, "Wow, I never thought I'd be able to do something like that." It was incredibly empowering for them.

The intern gained great experience from organizing and executing the entire event. That being said, it was a lot of work for

Christi, too. The intern had no experience organizing an event of that size, so Christi had to oversee his work and continually check his progress. But it was well worth it, in terms of member satisfaction and Christi's own satisfaction, helping her intern launch his fitness career.

OUR MEMBERS

One of the most fulfilling aspects of our business was serving our members. They were an incredible group of people who truly appreciated how we ran the club. Almost every day, we received compliments, and it inspired us to want to make things even better. Our members were the reason we were in business, and the community they built by referring friends and family was amazing. Without their support, it would never have been such a rewarding experience.

ELEVATE THE ORDINARY

- Before you start your business, make sure you have a solid financial plan. Do the homework to know your industry and understand how long it takes to generate a profit. Make sure you have the funds to see you through until that time.
- Be willing to take accountability. Do not go into business expecting to blame other people if things don't turn out the way you'd hoped and planned.
- Whenever you can, give back to your community. Doing so gets your name in the community. This is a great way to benefit your community while also enhancing your reputation.
- If you choose to run an internship program, make sure you have the proper setup to manage it. This might be some-

thing to look at further down the road, as your company grows. If you try to do it too early, you might not be in the best position to benefit the interns, your business, and your customers.

- Protect your company culture, so your customers feel appreciated by how you run your business.

CHAPTER EIGHT

GROWING! THE DECISION TO EXPAND (AGAIN)

OUTGROWING OUR SPACE

In 2003, we were in year seven, and it became clear to us that it was time to move. The gymnasts were outgrowing the ceiling height, and the cars were outgrowing the parking lot. It was time to get creative, and find a new space for our club.

We looked at numerous potential rental spaces. But most had lower ceiling heights than we needed for our gymnastics program. Or they had limited parking, which would have stunted our growth. We did finally find one space that had potential: 20,000 square feet in a plaza about a mile from our current location, along a busy highway. The rent was fifteen dollars per square foot, approximately twice what we were currently paying.

That space had possibilities, but we also had our eye on a three-and-a-half-acre plot of commercial land across the street from our current location. We calculated what it would cost to buy the land and construct a building that perfectly met our needs.

The final decision was based on research. When we looked at the cost, with CAM fees (i.e., common area maintenance) and everything else we'd spend, the new build would come out to about eight dollars per square foot. When we thought it all through, it made much more sense to buy land and build than to rent another existing space. Not only would it benefit our cash flow, but, more important-ly, owning versus renting would put us in a position to build equity for the long term. It was another big risk to take out a large mortgage to expand, but it would also give us many advantages over our com-petitors and the ability to control our overhead for the future.

The cost of the three and a half acres of land was $618,000. Our projected budget for the entire project, including the land, was $2.2 million.

SBA LOAN

We learned about a 504 Small Business Administration (SBA) loan that was designed for owner-operators like us. It required a 10% down payment ($220,000). The loan was backed by the federal gov-ernment, and 40% is provided by an SBA-certified development com-pany. All we had to do was find a bank willing to loan us the other 50%—and figure out the down payment. Once we had that all worked out, we'd be on our way to building equity, instead of paying rent.

We thought our local bank, with whom we had a relationship and who had seen us grow for the previous eight years, was the logical choice. Steve wrote a second business plan, full of optimism and growth projections. We thought it would be easy, but unfortu-nately, our application was turned down.

We went on to receive noes from three additional local banks. We were learning quickly that real estate development is *never* easy. Additionally, as we were aware, health clubs in general have a checkered past when it comes to sustainability. Finding a bank that was willing to take a chance on our ambitious plans turned out to be a tougher prospect than we'd expected.

This was a critical moment. We could have said, "This isn't going to work. We'll have to just rent again."

But the dream was still alive. The land was right across the street. Developing this property gave us a golden opportunity to significantly expand without, in essence, changing our location.

Steve says, "In my mind's eye, I could *see* the building over there. I told myself that we had to find a way. My head and my heart led me forward."

He searched online and found a company in Orlando that specialized in SBA 504 loans. They were a brokerage that matched entrepreneurs and private lenders. The broker offered to come to Vero Beach to meet with us.

Steve says, "The broker and I started talking about always learning and about the excitement of growing a business. It turns out he was a fan of *Good to Great* by Jim Collins, as I am. We had a wonderful conversation and built a strong rapport."

The broker lined up several potential lenders. After a mountain of paperwork and red tape, a bank in Utah offered us a loan. That was an exciting phone call to get!

When we took out our SBA loan, the government favored female owner-operators. Christi became our company CEO, with her ownership at 51% and Steve's at 49%.

BORROWING FROM FAMILY

We wouldn't have been able to take on the SBA loan if we couldn't show we had the down payment. Since we only had $50,000 on hand, which left $170,000 we needed to raise to get to the $220,000, it was time to get creative again.

We decided to ask Christi's father for the $170,000. This can be a tricky thing to do. Asking someone with whom you have a personal relationship if you can borrow money can be a big risk. What if they say no? What if you have trouble paying them back?

We didn't know the full extent of Christi's parents' finances, but we knew her dad had always been prudent. We were sure he wouldn't overextend himself to loan us money.

After much discussion, we decided to reach out to him with a proposal. We went in without expectation; we were comfortable with him saying no.

Most importantly, we'd thought through how we would repay him. We felt prepared to approach him as an investor, and we also wanted him to see a return on his investment. We crafted a written document that said that 5% of our net profit, after tax, would go to him every year. That money would then be held in an education fund, to be divided among his five grandchildren.

He loved the plan. He's a generous man, and he loved the idea of something extra for the greater good of the family, rather than just him receiving interest back on his investment.

At the time, Christi's siblings didn't know about the loan. Once the education fund was set up, they were told about the fund itself, but they didn't know how their dad was adding money to that account.

As it turned out, we were able to double the repayment amount we made to Christi's dad each month, because once we were in the new space, the business really took off. We paid him off in two and a half years, instead of five.

As the business grew each year, the 5% of the net after-tax profit grew, too. We enjoyed giving him that annual payment, and he enjoyed investing in his grandchildren's educations.

When we sold the business, he received 5% of the net sale. To be able to write him a check for an amount that paid a good chunk of each child's college education costs was very satisfying to us.

Christi's dad went out on a big limb for us. At that point, we had eight years of experience running the business and a successful track record—but still, it was a risk. We'll always be grateful to him that he was willing to take a chance on helping us grow.

THE POWER OF NEGOTIATING

The 20,000-square foot space in the plaza would have worked. We knew that, but we declined, because by then we had our hearts and minds set on developing the land.

"We'll go down to thirteen dollars a square foot," the landlord at the plaza told Steve.

"No, thanks," Steve replied. "We're pretty set on building our own place."

A month went by. We were still working on our SBA loan for buying and developing the land. But the plaza's landlord didn't know this. He called and said, "Look, we'll do twelve dollars a square foot."

"Thanks, but we really want to develop land," Steve told him.

Another month went by. The landlord called and said, "This is a big plaza. We have fifteen acres here. If you rent from us, we'll rename it 'Christi's Plaza.'"

By then, we'd gotten approval for our SBA loan. Steve came home and told Christi they were willing to rename the plaza after us. We admit it, we were tempted. But we wanted our own space, on our own terms, with the ability to build equity.

It was a lesson in negotiating. We learned that if you truly have a viable alternative, you might find out how low a price can go, and what other perks might get thrown in with the deal.

A REAL ESTATE DEVELOPER?

After we bought the land, a guy Steve knows said, "Oh, you're a real estate developer, too?"

"No, no, no," Steve replied. "A health club owner. We're just going to build a club."

The guy shook his head. "No," he said. "Now, you're a real estate developer."

We didn't know what he meant until we entered the development process. The challenges came one after another after another: red tape with the county, red tape with the SBA loan, a mitigation process. In the end, Steve was putting up fences and painting the entire inside of the facility himself.

CORNERSTONE OF FAITH

At around 11:00 p.m. on the night before the construction company was going to pour the slab for the new building across the street, Steve was closing our current gym. As he headed out to his car, a friend drove up.

Steve says, "This particular friend has always been encouraging. He'd tell me that God has big stuff ahead, if we are willing to lean into Him. He's usually pretty level headed, but that night he told me we *had* to go across the street and bury a Bible under the slab, near the location of the front doors."

Steve politely (but tiredly) declined, but the friend was determined. He grabbed an old Bible and a pocket knife from his car and started running toward the building site. Steve followed— mostly out of kindness, but also because he knew his friend would follow through on his plan with or without Steve.

"The next thing I know," Steve says, "I'm holding up a 4' by 8' section of wire mesh while he uses a four-inch pocket knife to 'dig' the hard-packed soil somewhere near where the front door will be. It was slow going, and I was starting to get annoyed. I was also thinking there better not be a slight hump by the front door that people might trip on."

It took a long time, but eventually the Bible was buried. The next day, the slab was poured. And, once we opened our doors, membership flourished.

"The experience taught me the importance of allowing others to follow their passion. Doing so can lead to something purposeful and enduring," Steve says. "I love reflecting back on the metaphor that the foundation of our business was literally built on the Bible."

WETLANDS MITIGATION

There were many challenges to developing the property. One of the biggest was that it was wetlands, and we had to mitigate it. If you're going to develop a wetland, you need to find another piece of property of equal size, then plant local species of vegetation on that alternative property. The idea is, if you're potentially displacing wildlife, you mitigate that displacement by providing a new habitat. You pay to have it developed with the species of plants and trees that occupied the space you're developing.

An environmental services company helps with the process. They locate an appropriate property and get approval from the county. They help you determine what needs to be planted, and help you find a service to do the planting. After you've had the vegetation planted, they go out and inspect, making sure the correct plants have been put in and any that are harmful to the area have been removed.

We received a commitment from the person selling us the property that he would take care of the mitigation process. But after we bought the property, he started dragging his feet. At that point, there was no real consequence to him. The mitigation would cost him money. He'd committed to paying for it and getting it done, but he was in no particular hurry.

We started getting notices from the county that the mitigation was not being done properly. The county said they'd shut down our construction if it wasn't taken care of immediately.

It seemed the previous owner of our land had financial problems or was trying to negotiate the minimum cost possible for the mitigation work. He was doing it piecemeal, and we had to keep putting pressure on him. Finally, after eight months of hounding him, it got done. But it was very stressful.

The lesson is to make sure you're in control of as many aspects of your own project as possible. In retrospect, we should have built the cost of a proper mitigation into the negotiated sale price for the land, and then worked with the environmental services company ourselves, instead of being at the mercy of our land's former owner.

THE PITFALLS OF COMMERCIAL DEVELOPMENT

When we were close to getting our Certificate of Occupancy (CO) for the new gym, a vendor we didn't go with for our windows called the county on us. He said the window over our front door was too big a plate of glass. He claimed it was against code and was subject to breaking in a storm. He told the county that we shouldn't be allowed to open with that window.

He only made that call because he was upset that he hadn't gotten our business. But it cost us. We had to wait weeks for the county to come out and test the glass. It turned out fine, and we received our CO, but it was a hassle and added a delay. It was a reminder to us of how we did *not* want to do business.

A similar problem arose over our general contractor. Steve gave our budget to the first general contractor he met with. He showed that contractor the architect's drawings. The contractor gave Steve verbal assurance that he could do the job within our budget, and Steve signed a contract with him.

When his bids came in, the total cost was $2.6 million—$400,000 over budget.

"We can't do this," Steve told the contractor. "We've gone as low as we can. We even had to borrow from family for the down payment. There's no way we can do 2.6."

"Okay," was all the contactor said.

Steve figured that was that. He shopped around, finding another contractor who could do the job within our budget. The slab was poured and we were on our way!

But before the slab had even cured, we received a letter in the mail from an attorney. The original general contractor was suing us for $100,000. He said Steve breached the contract by going with another general contractor. The contractor claimed he was owed $100,000 because that would have been his profit from the job.

Steve didn't understand it. When he'd told the contractor we couldn't do $2.6 million, the contractor simply said okay. He did not say we had any obligation to him.

We hired a lawyer and went to arbitration. We were able to negotiate a $21,000 settlement. We weren't happy about it, but we had to look at it as a 1% increase in our budget and let it go at that.

In retrospect, Steve shouldn't have signed that contract. He thought he and the contractor were acting together in good faith. But sometimes, that's not enough.

We all want to think everybody's on the up and up, but that's just not the case. With both the window vendor and the general contractor, we didn't expect retaliation, especially because we didn't feel we'd done anything wrong.

As business people and in all our relationships, we try to abide by the Golden Rule. But experiences like this remind us that not everyone does. All you can do is be realistic about what you're getting into, and have an attorney review contracts before you sign.

AN AMBITIOUS PLAN

One of the first things we did when we began to seriously plan for the development was to ask our members, "What do you want in the new club?"

As we planned and designed the new space, we took their requests into consideration. We were adding a pool. The new weight room would be significantly bigger. Our kids' gymnastics area would be substantially better.

We had an ambitious plan to open within nine months. This was especially ambitious because of the size of the new facility and the fact that we were putting in a pool. But we wanted it done quickly, because the interest on the construction loan would start after nine months. We'd have to start paying interest on the loan even if we weren't open.

We knew members would stay with us, because there was visual evidence that we were creating a bigger, better facility for them right across the street. As our members watched the new building going up, their eagerness grew. They wanted to be over there as much as we did!

And it wasn't just our members who were interested in the construction. People driving by turned to gawk, too. We put up a big sign that said, "Coming soon! The new Christi's Family Fitness Center." In a small town such as Vero Beach, a sign like that provides a huge marketing advantage.

By this time, we'd been in business eight years. We had traveling gymnastics teams. We had built up the membership, and we had a good name in the community. Everyone was excited!

WHAT HAPPENS WHEN WE "MAKE PLANS"

Finally, we had our CO in hand. We were ready to open our doors.

What happened next taught us much about "making plans." We believe God inspires us to tap into His vision, but He never wants us to own it. He lovingly teaches us that His plan has so much more to it, but in order to grab on to it, you actually need to let go of your own preconceived notions. He wants you to do it *together*—with Him and for Him.

So, what happened?

We received a weather report that a Category 3 hurricane was headed to Vero Beach. The eye of the storm was coming directly toward us. We had young kids and a house that wasn't all that new. We needed to get out of there.

We packed up the kids and started heading across the state to get away from the hurricane. Steve says, "As I was driving, I'm thinking, *I just poured every dollar, every ounce of sweat, and every bit of energy that I could muster to get that thing done—and now it could get blown down.*"

We hadn't even moved in. All our stuff was there, and everything was lined up to move across the street the following week.

We waited out the storm, Hurricane Francis, in a hotel on the other side of the state. A few days later, we made our way home, apprehensive about what we might find.

"I'll never forget turning the corner and seeing the building," Steve relates. "I'll never forget my enormous relief to see that it was still there."

There was damage, but it was minor. We felt God had smiled on us and blessed our "plans."

Not so fast.

Three weeks later, another weather report came in. A Category 2 hurricane was headed straight for Vero Beach.

"I was in denial," Steve says. "I didn't want to hear anyone talk about it. I couldn't believe we were going to get another one. Three weeks later, here comes another hurricane."

But again, we were fortunate. The damage to our building from the second hurricane was minimal. We were right down the street from the fire station, and because we were in the same power line as the fire station, our power came back on fairly quickly. We actually even slept at the gym with our kids the first couple of nights, because there was power at the gym but not at our house.

Vero Beach had never before been hit back to back by two hurricanes. A lot of people in our community didn't have electricity for several weeks afterward.

We became a bit of a haven for the community. Some of our members came in just to ask if we'd mind if they could take a shower. Of course, we didn't mind! We were happy to help out. There was a Comcast facility right next door to us. They asked if we'd allow their staff to come in and take showers and, again, we were happy to help.

Despite the hurricanes, we had an incredibly successful launch and grand opening. Membership grew the first year in the new facility by 35%. We think the sign out by the road during construction helped. Add in our new amenities and our reputation in the community, and people were flocking to the club.

GROWING OUR PROGRAMS

With so much more space in the new building, we had plenty of room to expand our services. Two of our most successful new programs were SilverSneakers and TRIBE Team Training™.

SILVERSNEAKERS

This national program, founded in the early 1990s, is designed to get seniors into gyms to improve their health, strength, and well-being. It focuses on both physical health and social interaction.

At Christi's, a staff member named Nancy Depp was in charge of SilverSneakers. Nancy's title was Senior Advisor, and her efforts were entirely focused on our senior market. She had a keen eye for what this demographic wanted and needed in a fitness center. She discussed her ideas with us before implementing them, but we approved almost every one of them.

Nancy put together health fairs in the middle of the day, which was when our senior members were typically in the gym. At these fairs, seniors could have their glaucoma and hearing checked, as well as having other health checks. Socially, Nancy organized a Christmas cookie exchange and other festive events throughout the year for our senior members.

Nancy also made connections within the local business community. She encouraged business owners to give a discount to our members when they showed their Christi's membership card at the business. This was a great way for us to network within that community. Christi's Fitness already had connections within the Vero Beach business community, but our SilverSneakers program actually became a community within that community.

For our SilverSneakers members, we uploaded their check-ins to a third party called Healthways, which was the channel between the insurance company and SilverSneakers. Healthways evaluated the check-ins, and we were paid for each visit.

This is another example of the advantage of long-term vision over short-term gain. We received three dollars for every Silver-Sneakers visit, with a cap of thirty dollars per month per member of the program. Our regular membership rate was twice that amount. For this reason, many other clubs kicked SilverSneakers to the curb. They assumed it wouldn't be worth it.

But we stuck with it. Because no other club had it, and because our variety of programs for seniors was far greater than any other club's, we became *the* club in Vero Beach for anyone interested in SilverSneakers.

We reasoned that most of our SilverSneakers members would not belong to Christi's without the SilverSneakers program—especially because our particular SilverSneakers program was run exceptionally well, by Nancy. We were not, in essence, losing money on those memberships, because this demographic would not have joined our club (or any club) if it wasn't for our SilverSneakers program.

After the first year with the program, we received about $1,000 a month, which isn't much, given the burden of running the program and the administrative costs. But we stuck with it, and its reputation grew within the Vero Beach senior community. More and more seniors joined the Christi's Fitness SilverSneakers program. It grew to $10,000 a month, which was unbelievable. Then it went to $15,000 a month, then $20,000. Eventually, we were making $30,000 a month from the program.

We ended up being one of the top generators of SilverSneakers revenue in the state of Florida. Our two-million-dollar mortgage, including property taxes and all our insurances, was more than covered by our Silver Sneakers program revenue.

We held all our classes for seniors in the middle of the day, from 11:00 a.m. to 2:30 p.m., when health clubs are typically very slow. Seniors had the flexibility to be in the club during those hours, something most working people did not. Nancy worked with our instructors to ensure they were offering classes tailored to Silver-Sneakers members during the middle of the day.

As for our other members, they seemed to enjoy having the SilverSneakers members in the facility. They could look at a senior working out and think, *hey, that person's older than I am, but I'm going to get there one day, and I want to be active like that, too.* Conversely, a SilverSneakers member seeing a little kid throwing a fit might think, *I was once that mother's age. I remember how hard it was, having little children—but what a blessing, too.*

Members who didn't like old people or young kids probably didn't want to be at Christi's Fitness in the middle of the day. And that was okay, too.

That being said, we wanted to make sure we didn't become a seniors-only facility. This was one of the reasons that in 2012, we went through a rebranding process with Don and two other employees: Rachel (whom you'll meet later in this chapter) and Trish. We needed their younger minds and younger ideas to help us tap into a younger market. We valued our seniors, but we also wanted young adult members. We wanted the facility to offer something for everyone.

TRIBE TEAM TRAINING

At one point, we brought in a small group training program called TRIBE Team Training. The program was introduced at a trade show we attended, and we really liked the concept. One of the largest clubs in Florida, located in Gainesville, was the first club in Florida to bring it in. Don and Christi went to Gainesville and met with the staff at that club. They took courses to learn all about the program, and we decided to introduce it at our club.

Don was in charge of our TRIBE Team Training program. He selected the staff members to be trained as coaches in the program.

Eventually, the TRIBE Team Training North American coaching director invited Don and one other of our staff to participate in a master training program. Once they completed the program, they were certified to teach others to be TRIBE coaches.

This was similar to what Christi had done for AAFA. These trainings were weekend work. There were huge benefits for Don and the other staff members, as well as for us. The recognition and the type of training they received, the knowledge about anatomy and physiology, represented a very high educational level within the fitness world.

For us, the benefit was that they could bring that knowledge back to the other TRIBE coaches at Christi's. And we advertised that the two of them were master trainers for this prestigious fitness organization.

REBRANDING TO ENTICE A YOUNGER MARKET

In 2012, we hired a young woman named Rachel as part of our marketing team. You'll hear more from Rachel in her own words later in this chapter.

Rachel was part of the team that helped us rebrand the gym. We'd started as Christi's Fitness and Weight Management, and then we became Christi's Family Fitness. Now, fifteen years after starting the business and eight years after moving to the new facility, it was time to freshen our image.

At that point, our SilverSneakers program was booming, and our children's programs were thriving. While "family" certainly fit our model, we also wanted to appeal to a younger, hipper client. Rachel helped us change the club's name to Christi's Fitness and freshen our logo, marketing materials and website.

Rachel was young, and she had a vision that appealed to people in her age demographic. This goes back to what we said earlier, about hiring people who see things from a different point of view than your own. When we saw how smart and dynamic Rachel was, we thought, *we're going to listen to this woman, because she sees the world differently than we do.*

As a business owner, it's imperative that you have the ability to do that. You have to check your ego at the door and realize you don't have all the answers. With Rachel, we had the wherewithal to listen to her, and our brand vastly improved because of it.

IMPROVEMENTS AND MAINTENANCE

Steve had always been bothered by an editorial comment in our local paper about the appearance of our metal building just after it was finished. Someone wrote how unhappy she was with the aesthetics of our building. She said, "It looks like a barn."

She did have a point. It was a long, rectangular metal building, with the same roof height and pitch throughout. Steve says, "But after borrowing $2,200,000 and aging myself about five years during nine months of construction, I found it tough to swallow a comment like that."

Eight years after the building was constructed, the outside needed some minor repairs and painting. Estimates for just painting were about $60,000, which was more than we had in reserves.

Steve looked into an exterior "renovation system" that would provide additional insulation and make the outside look like concrete construction with a stucco finish. This process would cost $250,000.

That amount seemed unattainable. Steve went to our bank and explained the details to them. They agreed we could pull out some equity and refinance to get it done.

We looked at this as an investment, not an expense. Our reasons were as follows:

- The insulation benefit would save us $500 to $750 per month on our utility bill.
- The new look of the building would align with our goal of being the premium heath club in the county.
- As it had been when we originally constructed the building, the marketing effect of the construction project would be powerful in our small community.
- The enhanced appearance of the building would increase the value of our investment when the time came to sell.

A lot of people wouldn't spend that kind of money on an exterior when the exterior was fine (other than being a metal building and needing a paint job). But we knew there was great value in making our club look more upscale.

In 2014, we won an Architectural Recognition Award from the Indian River County Chamber of Commerce for Commercial Building Renovation. So, it seems we weren't the only ones who thought that investment paid off!

KEEP TAKING RISKS

In any business, risk-taking should be a given. Trying a new program, expanding your space, or upgrading your equipment and facility should be part of your culture. Successful businesses have a culture of stepping out in faith, serving their customers, and getting outside their comfort zones.

When you continually reinvest in your business, people see you as trustworthy, successful, and financially stable. During our business life, we always took chances that helped us toward our goal of being the highest-quality club in our area. While we had our ups and downs, we never regretted looking at things differently and sometimes going out on a limb. Our business thrived because we were willing and eager to do that.

———

"Disciplined runners consistently clear their heads and focus fully on the journey ahead... because their passion and zeal for the goal supersedes the strain. The goal beckons them onward. Passion doesn't negate weariness; it just resolves to press beyond it."
– Priscilla Shirer

———

MEET AN EMPLOYEE: RACHEL'S STORY

My job at Christi's was to implement marketing techniques for bringing in new members and retaining members. I never interviewed for the job. I was a new mom, but I wanted to work part time, so I got a Pilates certification. We were moving to Vero Beach, and I emailed Christi's to inquire about teaching Pilates there.

I sent my resume, which included my marketing experience. Christi responded by saying we could talk when I got to town, but in the meantime, she was forwarding my resume to Steve, because he might need some help with marketing.

All I wanted to do was teach Pilates classes. I went in thinking, *I don't know if I even want this marketing job.*

I later learned that Steve had already decided to hire someone else, but had not yet extended an offer. But he'd said he would meet with me, and he followed through on that. After he and I talked, he offered me the job. I appreciated the culture at the facility, so I decided to take it.

I'd been there about a year when we decided to rebrand and drop the "Family" segment from the name. I worked with Don, the general manager, and with Trish, another coworker at Christi's who taught group exercise classes and also worked with us on marketing. I'd lived in New York, and Trish is from Miami, so we both came from environments where things were a bit more hip. We wanted to bring that image to the club.

Trish and I were the target market: young mothers with some disposable income. We were working, but not full time, so we were flexible. Moms are powerful, because they talk, and word of mouth is the best marketing tool.

The branding for Christi's Family Fitness featured a character who looked like Gumby. He wasn't Gumby, but he looked like him, and he was everywhere. I felt the character didn't mesh with the modern, sleek image we were going for. I really wanted "Gumby" out, but I was nervous about approaching Steve and Christi.

But they were very receptive to letting the character go. Steve and Christi knew that the best ideas come when not everybody's in agreement. Why hire someone if you're not going to engage their strengths?

We changed the look of the brochures, making them sleeker and more streamlined. Steve and Christi brought in a graphic designer, and it became a full-time job for her because we had so much for her to do.

Steve and Christi wanted youth. They wanted freshness. They were fifteen years older than us, and they wanted our ideas. None of us wanted to completely overhaul everything; we just wanted the club's image to evolve. It was already working beautifully, but it could be elevated. Steve and Christi initiated the rebranding, then let us run with it.

As entrepreneurs, Christi and Steve were role models for my husband, John, and me. I admired how they worked as a team and how resourceful they were.

When you have an idea for a business, you're going to hear "no" a lot. Friends, parents, other businesspeople will say your idea isn't going to work.

John is a veterinarian, and he wanted to bring affordable, preventative pet healthcare to Vero Beach. We're both also conservation-minded, and we envisioned a business in which a portion of the profits was donated to conservation projects.

Knowing how Christi and Steve's community-focused business model generated success, I thought our approach had merit. But there were already eighteen veterinary clinics in our small town. We were told it would never work. Nonetheless, we felt strongly about our vision, and we opened Community Veterinary Clinic. Within four years, we had 4,000 clients and a great reputation in Vero Beach.

We've built a community. We followed through on our commitment to affordable pet care and conservation, and we make sure our customers know that. We've found that generosity breeds generosity: people come into our clinic, hear someone's story, and offer to pay for their dog's treatment. It's amazing, looking beyond numbers and bricks and mortar to see that you're making a contribution to the community. That really is the biggest gift.

Starting a business is both exciting and terrifying. But I'd always figured you walk in and things just work out, right from the start. Very rarely, I've learned, does that actually happen. In our first year, we lost a lot of money. Christi and Steve had had a similar experience, but they persevered and became successful, which was inspiring. John and I kept at it, and in our most recent year, we had revenue of a million dollars.

The first time we had to fire someone, we were devastated. When we told Christi and Steve about it, they said, "You can't change people. If it's not the right fit, you've got to protect your community. You need to move on, and do it quickly." They said that letting the person go was the kinder thing to do, rather than trying to limp along, with nobody happy.

It's important for any businessperson to articulate mission and vision. You need to know what you're trying to do and what the purpose is. But you also need to know *how* to get things done. There's purpose and direction, but there's also the means to accomplish it. At Christi's—and at Community Veterinary Clinic—that's where I came in.

ELEVATE THE ORDINARY

- Expanding your business is exciting, but a business plan is essential to make sure it is feasible.
- Borrowing money from a family member can be risky. If it doesn't work out, it can break up a family. Make sure to approach it as a business transaction and have a written plan for paying your family member back.
- Research as many options as possible, before negotiating any contract or large purchase.
- In any business transaction, retain as much control as you can. While we all want to trust others, it's important to do thorough research, make sure everything is in writing, and spend the money on appropriate professionals to guide you through any process you're unfamiliar with.
- Consider not just short-term gains, but also long-term investments. Sometimes, it can take some vision to see the long-term gain in something that initially seems like it won't pay off.
- Don't be afraid to periodically update your brand. When rebranding, make sure to work with professionals who understand your target customers' demographics.

CHAPTER NINE

Ties That Bind: Our Business, Our Marriage, Our Faith

GETTING TESTED

We touched on this earlier, but it bears repeating: Christi and Steve have very different, but complementary work styles. That's a strength, but there were also moments when it created challenges in our business and our relationship.

Christi is very intentional, not only with her commitments, but also with her personal time. When we owned the club, Christi would schedule personal time. This might involve getting a massage, getting her nails done, or meeting a friend for lunch. She also organized family events and kept track of our kids' school events. She's always used a calendar. She likes being able to see her whole calendar and create a balance within her schedule.

Steve, on the other hand, was (and still is) more spontaneous. He enjoys running in the morning and playing tennis once or twice a week, but he doesn't always schedule it.

When we owned the club, Steve was there a lot of the time. Because of Christi's scheduling, Steve was often pulled into family and school activities, which helped him be less of a workaholic.

Without that, he would have gone from one thing at the club to the next, to the next, to the next.

Steve always admired Christi's efficiency and productivity. He says, "I'd think, *wow, she's doing a lot*. It motivated me to do even more."

"I felt that we were both incredibly invested in the business," Christi says. "It never felt to me like one of us was carrying more of a load than the other. I think it's because we concentrated on different areas of the business, too."

Steve was more focused on the relational side of things and smoothing over issues with people. Christi, on the other hand, was systematic. Steve says, "I appreciate her skills. You can *kumbaya* all day long, but you can't run a business solely that way. In our gym, there were lesson plans, safety certifications, progressions in gymnastics, training to show coaches how to progress kids, and a myriad of other practical aspects that had to be addressed continually. Thankfully, Christi stayed on top of that, which gave me plenty of time for the kumbayas."

Christi adds, "Of course, to run a successful business, it's also important to keep employees and customers happy—something Steve did very well. This is why we made a great team."

RUNNING A BUSINESS WITH YOUR SPOUSE

If we're making it sound easy, rest assured that it was not. Owning the business together puts a lot of stress on our marriage; it definitely complicates things.

Our different styles could be problematic in our marriage, because if we weren't careful, the result was disconnection. Steve says, "If I had free time, instead of thinking about some fun thing I could be doing with Christi, I'd think, *oh, I can take care of this thing at the gym.* I needed her planning and scheduling in order to keep me in check."

That's one of the pitfalls of being in business with your spouse. It's actually, in its own right, a pitfall of being an entrepreneur. For some people, it's easy to become a bit obsessed. Christi didn't do that, but Steve did.

In all those years, we never missed any of our children's events. Ninety percent of the time, we were both there. Both of our kids were on travel sports teams, both played instruments, and both were involved in other activities in middle school and high school.

Christi explains, "When the kids got to those ages, I said to Steve that I didn't want to be in the gymnastics room every day from three o'clock until six thirty. Before that point, I was in the gymnastics room every afternoon, Monday through Thursday. I told Steve I wanted to pick up our kids up from school every day. I wanted that time with them."

Steve agreed, and we did a big search for someone who could manage those key hours in the gymnastics room. We brought in a husband and wife, Jeff and Jill Gothard, to team-coach. They were extremely knowledgeable, responsible, and caring. We paid a much bigger salary than we would have if Christi had been in the room supervising. But it was worth it. Christi didn't want to miss those moments with our kids, and Steve was on board with that.

That being said, a family business is inevitably hard on children. It's almost impossible not to bring the work home, no matter how you juggle your time and how devoted you are to your family.

Our daughter, Jordan, in particular got sick of us talking about the business. Looking back, we can hardly blame her. Our conversations at home about the club weren't much fun for our kids.

COMMUNICATION IS KEY

We were business partners, but we also always had to remember that first and foremost, we were husband and wife, mom and dad. We always tried to communicate with each other on both a personal level and a business level.

When we were considering the idea of opening a fitness center, Steve prayed about it. He was looking for direction from God about whether going into business together was a good idea. Around this time, he heard a radio program that highlighted the positives of working with your spouse. It explained that one of the best parts would be that we'd both know what each other was going through every day. We'd have each other to lean on for difficult decisions, and we would be equally responsible with the business finances. This was the encouragement Steve needed to move forward.

STRIVING FOR BALANCE

_____

"If you don't set your own agenda, somebody else will. If I didn't fill my schedule with things I felt were important, other people would fill my schedule with things they felt were important."
– Melinda Gates

_____

One thing we learned about early on was intentionality. The reality is that most of us, if we love what we're doing, could easily work 24/7. We knew that, and we were sometimes tempted by it (especially Steve). There were moments where we both had to do that kind of push, but if we were not intentional about our time and our priorities, it could have become all the time.

When we built balance into our lives, it actually made us more effective when we were focusing on work. If things were running smoothly in the other areas of our lives, we were happier, and we had more energy to put into the business during working hours.

We tried to create a balance between running a business together and raising children together. We were intentional about connecting with our kids and not devoting all of our time to the business.

For instance, we made an intentional decision that our kids weren't just going to hang out at the gym all day long. Christi's mom was a big help. Early on, she'd come to our house to watch the kids twice a week. Other days, we worked it out between the two of us. If Christi had to be at the gym teaching a class, then Steve had the kids. If Christi wasn't teaching, then she might have the kids while Steve was at the gym. We did a lot of alternating back and forth with our children.

We did use the nursery at the gym when they were little, especially in the mornings. But we didn't want them there in the evenings. They needed to be at home, having their dinner and their baths, playing, getting to bed on time—in other words, having a normal kid existence.

We learned we had to sacrifice some financial gain to create balance. If we focused on saving every dollar and not adding to payroll, we would be losing out on time with family and friends.

Below are several other examples of how we fostered work/life balance while running our club.

MIDDAY CLOSURE

As discussed earlier, initially when we opened the gym, we only had group exercise and kids' gymnastics programs. In those years, we were open during the peak hours in the morning, about 8:00 to 11:30 a.m. We would completely close in the middle of the day, then open back up from 4:00 to 7:00 p.m.

We felt this was well worth it, for the balance it gave us. But it was a sacrifice. There were people who came to the club during our "closed" hours, and we're sure some of them were surprised to find the doors locked and no one inside. We might have lost potential customers who came to check out our place. But for us, for our family when our kids were little, it was important to do things this way.

CLOSING ON SUNDAYS

In the fitness industry, Sunday is the slowest day. Still, over the years, people told us they'd love to join our club but they couldn't because we were not open on Sundays and that was the only day they had available to work out at a gym.

But we stayed committed to our policy. Sunday was our family day. We were (and are) churchgoers, and it was important for us to have a day set aside for that. It connected us with our faith.

This is another example of making a tradeoff. We knew we were sacrificing business to gain personal time that was important to us.

On the flip side of prospective members who wanted us to open on Sundays were many existing members who appreciated our "closed on Sundays" policy. "Good for you," they'd tell us. These were people who lined up philosophically with us, and that helped us feel good about the tradeoff we were making.

When you own a business, it's hard to turn off your mind, even at home. You think of a million things you could be doing at work. We still thought about work on Sundays, but with the gym closed, at least we knew we weren't going to get interrupted with a phone call on that day.

We maintained our "closed on Sundays" policy until 2004, when we opened the new facility. At that point, we were growing so much, it made sense to open on Sundays. We also had more staff by then, including managers who could handle the club on Sundays, allowing us to continue having it as a church and family day.

We survived our "closed on Sundays" decision, and maybe even thrived from that decision, in terms of family. Our children gained the biggest benefit. Those Sundays together as a family were precious to us.

TRADING OFF WITH OTHER PARENTS

During the first three years we owned the club, when it wasn't making money, we found a way to escape by trading off with our next-door neighbors. We'd take their three kids at our house for a sleepover on Friday night, allowing them to do whatever they wanted: go out to dinner, go to Orlando, or just have dinner at their house and stay in. Then, on Saturday night, all five kids (ours and theirs) would go to their house, giving us much-needed couple time.

As we began making more money, we made this a bit more elaborate, with two-night getaways, usually somewhere else within the state. But the childcare tradeoff remained the same. It gave us peace of mind, knowing our kids were happy, having fun, and safe next door. And it was gratifying to be able to do the same for our neighbors.

We hosted a lot of sleepovers at our house. We did a lot of driving for our kids' travel teams. We'd take five kids in our car whenever we could. We wanted our kids' friends around us as much as possible, so we could get to know who our kids were spending their time with.

GETAWAYS WITH OUR KIDS

During year four, which was our break-even year, we began to occasionally book a hotel with our kids in West Palm Beach, an hour away. Our kids called it "the swan motel." (It was actually an Embassy Suites that had swans in a pond on its property.) Roughly once a quarter, we went there for the weekend. Even though we were only an hour away and it was only a couple of nights, it was very freeing for all four of us.

A CONSCIOUS EFFORT TO LIVE MODESTLY

We lived very modestly, in an 1,800-square foot home. It was our starter home, from the start of the business all the way until we sold Christi's Fitness. As the business became more successful, there were times when we thought about buying a bigger house. But we chose to spend our money on experiences with our children, rather than living in a bigger home. The kayak, the jet ski, the hot air balloon, the dune buggy rides, the Segway—we did all those things with our kids. We rented boats; we did ziplining. We traveled all over the world. It was intentional to spend our money in this way, rather than on a bigger home.

The other advantage of staying in the same home for many years was that it built up equity. We were able to refinance our home twice to be able to fund things for the business.

Beginning in year five of running the business, we hired a housekeeper to come every other week and clean our house. As in many homes, before we hired a cleaner, most of these tasks had fallen to the female head of household. Christi says, "I decided it was better to pay someone to clean my house than to spend my free time doing that. The housekeeper was an added expense, but this expense bought me time with my kids, which was much more important."

NOT EVERY BUSINESS PARTNERSHIP IS A MATCH

Toward the end of running the agricultural company, Steve had a business partner. The partner was a driven, Type A personality; he came in early and stayed late. Steve was more of a "regular hours" type of guy. Steve's partner felt the arrangement was unequal, because he worked so many hours. But Steve didn't want to spend that much time at work, especially in those days, when it was work he wasn't passionate about. They ended it amicably, because they both realized they were not a good fit.

We have many friends who have been in business with a partner, and one of them ended up buying out the other at some point. Watching others go through these experiences, and remembering Steve's experience with his partner, has made us all the more appreciative of how our work styles meshed so well with one another's. It's a lot of the reason we were able to build a successful business together, over the span of more than two decades.

THE ROLE OF FAITH

A huge aspect that shaped our partnership, both in marriage and in business, is our shared beliefs.

Christi grew up in a Presbyterian church, but was also exposed to many other denominations. Her religious experiences gave her a strong belief in Jesus and the Bible. Growing up, Steve attended a Trinitarian Church with his family, which gave him a belief that Jesus, God, and the Holy Spirit are one.

For many years, we have been members of a nondenominational church that simply teaches the Word of the Bible. When our kids were little, we did devotionals with them in their beds at night. They went to a private Christian school until high school, at which point they attended and graduated from our local public school.

Our shared faith is an important part of our lives as a couple and in our family. It infused our business partnership, too.

We don't push our faith on other people, but if they see it in our lives and ask us about it, we talk about it with them. We've had many conversations with employees, club members, and friends about our faith. We're always happy to discuss what we've learned and what we share with each other.

OUR BELIEFS SAW US THROUGH

We'll be perfectly honest here: there were some rocky roads along the way, both in business and in our personal lives. It was intense, at times. It was then that faith saw us through.

"Early in our marriage," Steve explains, "I broke Christi's trust. I used drugs and alcohol—kind of holdover behavior from college, when I was a partier. I began hiding my drinking and drug usage from Christi. But, of course, she knew something was up. I wasn't home, or I was coming home late. And I was making excuses."

Christi says, "I could tell that I was afterthought for him. And I knew this wasn't the way a marriage is supposed to be."

"At thirty-one," Steve goes on, "I was at a very low point in my life, abusing alcohol and drugs. I was disappointed in myself, disappointed that I hadn't been able to leave all that behind, the college life. I was still caught up in the party scene, but ironically, it was actually very lonely. I had a lot of despair about what I'd been doing during this first year of our marriage. I remember thinking, *I know God didn't put me here to do this. He certainly didn't have me take vows at the altar with my wife, only to have this kind of marriage.*"

Steve went to AA for a few months, then transitioned into a church-based accountability group. He kept up with the group for over eighteen years. He was able to successfully stay off the drugs and alcohol while raising our kids and building the business.

In those years, we were focused on the club and the kids. But Steve was a worrier, and his anxiety came out through his intense focus on the business, rather than on our family.

He says, "Instead of paying attention to my wife in my free time, I'd be thinking about the gym and all the things I could be doing if I were there. Our Sundays off, our getaways, and everything else we did to create balance were, in theory, great ideas. But while we were together, either just the two of us or with the children, I wasn't always connecting. Instead, often I was thinking about the club."

A STEP BACKWARD

Things took a turn for the worse when Steve's mother died of a brain hemorrhage, followed soon afterward by the death of one of his sisters, who succumbed to breast cancer. Mourning the losses made this a very difficult time for Steve. Eventually, he got to the point where he felt like he needed to get away and forget about everything. He says, "I kept thinking about the partying I'd done when I was younger. I just wanted to feel like that again."

He decided to drive to Miami and party—just a little bit, he told himself. Just as a release from the pressures and the grief.

One time turned into another. And then another, and another.

As he'd done when he was younger, Steve hid his partying from Christi. He always came home. Sometimes, he drank in the house, but he hid his alcohol so Christi wouldn't know about it. A couple of times, he was sick as a result of drinking too much. He told Christi he had the flu.

During this time, there was also pornography involved. Steve had been introduced to pornography in his home, as a young boy.

It stayed with him, and as the internet progressed, he dabbled in it, even though he knew it created another wedge between Christi and himself.

Of course, eventually she figured it out. At that point, Steve went back to AA, thinking alcohol was the root of the problem. He says, "I went for a few months, but I didn't identify as an alcoholic, and I realized it wasn't really helping my marriage, because the trust had been broken again."

We decided we needed counseling. The counselor talked with us about how when two flawed people (and we are all flawed people, in one way or another) come together, it doesn't eliminate the flaws. He said that our self-worth and identity needed to come from God, not from the other person.

He told us, "If you expect all your needs to be met by this other person and expect that this is how you'll have a happy marriage, eventually you find it doesn't work."

That was a tough pill to swallow. We kept trying to work through it, but even with the counseling, we were not doing well. Christi says, "A relationship is built on trust, but at that point, there was no trust. So it felt like there was no relationship. I had no idea where to go from there."

"EVERY MAN'S BATTLE"

Then one day, Christi heard a radio show that talked about a conference called "Every Man's Battle." The conference was designed to address the pornography addiction that grips so many men. It was in Atlanta. A Christian organization was putting on the conference, and it was expensive. But Christi told Steve about it, and they agreed he should go.

Steve says, "At the conference, I learned that it really wasn't about pornography, alcohol, or drugs, per se. It was about the hiding. It was about the secrecy. I had lived a life of hiding not just substance abuse, but also my negative feelings. I thought people would like me better, would love me more, if I always exuded positivity."

At the conference, participants were encouraged to go home and reveal to their wives everything that their wives didn't know about their past. Steve says, "Some of the guys said to me, 'I'm not going to do that—are you?' I replied, 'Well, I need to.'"

The conference leaders advised having someone like your wife's sister or mother be there, in case she needed a third party to break down with when you revealed your news. Steve says, "Hearing that really drove home the magnitude for me. I was able to put myself in Christi's shoes and imagine what it would be like for her, hearing everything I had to tell her."

It was suggested that participants write everything down on the plane ride home, which Steve did. At home, he revealed everything to Christi.

"I thought my marriage was over. There was so much I hadn't shared with her, and I was so embarrassed and ashamed," Steve says. "But there was also was a sense of relief. I wasn't hiding anymore. There was a freedom in that, painful though it was. I told Christi, and I also told our kids. Christi wanted me to do that. They were older by this time, no longer little kids. It was hard for them to hear, but they deserved to know."

Steve goes on, "I felt like the worst failure in the world."

OPENING OUR HEARTS

Amazingly, Christi was willing to try working through it with Steve. We were honest with one another. We prayed—a lot.

Still, we couldn't figure out a way forward. We would ask each other, "Can you see a way through this?" We pretty much came up empty.

It took some time, but a willingness to ask God for help put us on a path of unselfishness versus selfishness. When we prayed, our eyes and hearts were opened. We realized it wasn't just about making each other happy, whether we stayed together or split up. It was more about what God wanted us to do. Once we came to a realization that both of us felt strongly that God wanted us to work through it, we were able to slowly begin rebuilding trust.

Throughout the next ten years, our relationships with God grew tremendously, both individually and as a couple. We've been able to see His love poured out in each of us, as individuals and through the amazing process of reconnection.

Steve made a covenant with Christi that if he drank, he would drink one or two beers, and if he drank more than that, he would tell her. If he did any kind of a drug or looked at pornography, he would tell her. He explains, "Just making that covenant gave me freedom from bondage to alcohol, drugs, and pornography. Since the conference, I haven't used pornography. I learned that I was in bondage to secrets, and it just manifested itself in those elements."

For a long time afterward, Christi had her guard up. "But it was what I needed," Steve says. "I had to unconditionally love her, and I had to be willing to endure whatever she was feeling and take steps to improve our relationship, even if I didn't always feel good about it. I'm such an emotional, feeling person. During the slow process of reconnection, there were times when there was very little emotion coming from Christi to me. That was painful, but it was exactly what I needed at the time."

Christi adds, "Looking back, it might have felt good for me to leave, but it would have been devastating for our children, our family, and our business. I decided it would be selfish on my part to not even *try* to work it out, to just throw everything away. I admit that I did think that perhaps, down the road, when the kids were older and we no longer owned the business, we might get divorced. But Steve and I were so connected and involved—with our family, our community, our church. I thought about what it would be like if we eventually had other spouses. Our kids would have their own kids, and they would have to coordinate time with each of us, without the other one there. What a strain on them!"

She goes on, "Beyond that, Steve and I always had respect in the way we speak with each other. We were never screamers or yellers. Despite everything that happened, there were still so many things we truly loved about each other and enjoyed about being together. I could always see the good in him, everything I loved about him, even though there were other things I didn't like at all."

Christi concedes that Steve probably felt like he wasn't getting much from her when he was trying to be honest and open up. She says, "I spoke with my family and a couple of very tight, close friends about it. And Steve and I continued with the counseling. But otherwise, I kept it private. I certainly knew it wasn't appropriate to blab it all over the place at the club."

After we got through this experience, there were times when we shared parts of it with certain staff members, especially some of our leaders. This was in order to help them in their own relationships. Learning about trust and honesty are important in any relationship, whether personal or business. If our staff and leaders could gain insight by hearing about our experience, we were willing to be vulnerable and share it.

And that's exactly why we've shared it here, too.

AN OPPORTUNITY TO LEARN

We were fortunate that Steve's issues did not affect the business too much. If he'd been the one doing all the planning and organization, it likely would have been different. But because Steve's specialty was taking care of relationships, he was able to continue doing that, despite the secrets and the difficulties within our own relationship.

Christi says, "Steve is very spontaneous, creative, and resourceful. He thrives on hands-on, relationship-based work. If it had been me, I wouldn't have been able to function as well. I'm much more structured and organized, and my type of task-driven work would have been very difficult for someone who was also abusing, hiding, and lying."

The experience only reinforced what we already knew: our different personalities and styles made us great partners. What a waste it would have been, if we'd ended up throwing it all away!

These days, when talking about what happened, Steve says, "I see so much more in her. I love her more every day. Christi inspired me to put it out in the light. And I have to give glory to

God for it, because He truly opened my heart up and inspired me, too."

The reality is, we're human, and none of us are perfect. Sometimes we stumble. But there's a way to recover. It doesn't need to be the end of the story.

This is what we learned, once we reached the other side of those challenging times.

MEET A MEMBER: LAURA

I met Christi at another club where she taught. Back then, she was the "new girl on the block." Seeing someone so secure and together made an impression on me. You feel a real connection when someone like that teaches a fitness class.

One night, I had a very vivid dream, featuring walls being broken down and a high ceiling. New rooms were being made. I saw myself in this huge room, working out, and yet, there was rubble. The dream gave me the sense that something was being built. Then, I heard talk in this dream: "Meet Christi's Fitness. You want to go there."

Given that, it's probably no surprise that when Steve and Christi opened their club, I started taking classes there. Right away, I felt such respect for how they were running their business. I felt a vibe of family togetherness. There was an energy that you don't get in a corporate, chain gym. I experienced connection at a deep soul level, throughout all the years I was a member there.

When they were just starting out, when they were owners of this very modest gym, I saw so much goodness coming from that. I was inclined to encourage it, so I decided to write them a note. I was a little hesitant, because I didn't really know them. But I needed to express what I felt, because it was so positive. I told them about my dream. I felt it was significant and that it was from the Lord. I tend to write better than I speak, so I wrote about it in my note to Steve and Christi.

When two people are building something together and are creating this beautiful playground, that feels good. Christi's Fitness was my escape; it was my way to be on the playground.

I'll be honest: when I first moved here, I kind of hated Vero Beach. I'm from Hawaii. Coming to Vero Beach, it felt flat and dead. In Hawaii, we talk about having "aloha." It's a greeting, but it also means love, peace, and compassion. I didn't feel much aloha in Vero Beach, until I started meeting people like Christi, Steve, and the staff and members at their gym.

It was real. It felt like family, like a gathering place. It wasn't just a place you go to get on the elliptical, do your workout, then get out as soon as you can.

I have four kids. Moselle, my youngest, is friends with Christi and Steve's daughter, Jordan. Moselle was a dancer and a gymnast. She took classes at Christi's, and she worked there a little bit, too.

Another daughter, Arial, came to classes with me sometimes. I remember one time when we were leaving the gym. Steve came out to the car. He said to her, "Arial, why do you come to the gym?"

She looked at him and said, "Because I don't want to get fat."

I don't think that was the answer Steve was looking for! But there's something to be said about the owner of the club coming outside and engaging us in conversation. It represents what they created at the club. It was an extension of their home and their lives.

Since they sold the club, it's not the same. But Christi still teaches there; her presence is there. And I love seeing Steve when he comes in. I go to the gym several times a week. I love the classes that Christi teaches, and there are a few others I enjoy, too.

My husband, Michael, and I run an educational project, called Project Ezra, in Nicaragua and Honduras, along the Coco River, which creates the border between those countries. We work with Miskito Indians to provide school buildings and materials, and train teachers. Michael first went down there in 1984 to help with relief efforts after the Sandinista government of Nicaragua took control of the Miskito people. Thousands of refugees escaped across the river to Honduras. The war ended in 1990, and the refugees returned to Nicaragua. Since then, Project Ezra has grown in scope and quality.

To support our work, we opened a café in Vero Beach, called the Rio Coco Café. Michael had some wonderful photographs he'd taken of the Rio Coco, and Steve helped us find someone to turn them into huge wallscapes for our café walls. It was sort of replicating what Steve did with the wallscapes in the gym. He helped us do that in our café, and it made all the difference for us.

We've since opened a second location in Vero Beach. We have a location in Honduras, too.

These days, we socialize with Steve and Christi. It's turned into a friendship. We've gained a lot of good tips and inspiration from them. I loved their little touches at the gym, like remembering staff birthdays, and we've tried to emulate that.

At our cafés, Michael and I err on the side of getting too personal with our employees, and that can create issues. One piece of advice Steve and Christi gave us was to create boundaries. They even do that in their personal lives. When Christi and I get together, she'll say something like, "Okay, I have one hour, because I have to pick up Jordan." And she sticks with it.

For Michael and me, that's a good lesson. We both tend to be all over the place, tend to go with the flow. We tend to be more spontaneous. Christi's example has been really good for me.

When they were running their club, Christi and Steve always tried to be one step ahead of everything. As a member, I felt satisfaction being in a place like that. It showed me that they cared.

It's inspired us in our business, as well. We're not just serving coffee in our cafés, we're creating community. If we can keep it right here—in relationships with each other, with our family, with our staff and our customers—then the world will know us by the love we have for each other. To me, that's the meaning of success.

ELEVATE THE ORDINARY

- Before you go into business with someone else, think about how your personalities work together. For some people, it might be better to have a sole proprietorship.
- It's important to have a life beyond your business. Your business can suffer if you don't take time away from it.
- If you have a family, how will you make sure their needs are balanced with the needs of your business?
- Think about how you deal with stress. Realize that as a business owner, you will likely be experiencing more stress than you do when you work for someone else. Make sure that appropriate, healthy coping mechanisms for dealing with stress are built into your lifestyle.

- If you're experiencing crisis in a relationship, whether personal, business, or both, what resources do you have for getting through the crisis? As a business owner, you need to make sure you'll be able to manage the unexpected (but inevitable) crises that come your way.

CHAPTER TEN

THE END OF AN ERA: SELLING CHRISTI'S FITNESS

AT A CROSSROADS

The parking lot was full. The classes had waiting lists. We'd just celebrated our thirteenth anniversary in the new building, but we hadn't expanded since we added our boutique studio, Studio C, across the street in our old rental space. Was it time to add more space again? We figured it was.

We got a quote from a contractor for adding 5,000 square feet on the west end of the existing structure. With design, construction, county fees, interior modifications, and equipment, the total projected cost was over $1 million.

Based on a conservative growth forecast, a return on investment would take ten years. And we still had a mortgage on the initial purchase of the land and construction of the building.

After much discussion, we decided it would be wiser to sell while the business was peaking, rather than take on additional debt to expand. We had several key reasons for making this decision:

- Our business was thriving, but we still had to compete with the seemingly endless proliferation of new fitness ventures in our area. It felt like new facilities were opening every month. And we did not foresee any decrease in competition.

206 • CHRISTI AND STEVE WADE

- Our staff had grown to over a hundred people, and managing a staff of that size was much more time consuming than it had been when our staff was smaller.
- Running our children's programs had become a challenge, especially in terms of retaining quality part-time staff.
- The $1 million expansion would be necessary if we wanted to keep growing our business, but that number was substantial. At the same time, our current space was limiting our potential to grow the membership and see a return on any upcoming investments.
- Expansion possibilities aside, our aging building would need capital improvements and considerable investment in maintenance projects in the near future.

HAVING AN EXIT STRATEGY

By the time we made the decision to sell, we were ready for it, in more ways than one. Our readiness was due to planning for it long before we decided it was time to sell. We had an exit strategy that proved valuable, and we'd created that exit strategy very early on in running our club. Simply put, our goals for the club were always tied to our exit strategy.

Our exit strategy involved several key factors.

Financials. We'd always known we would sell at some point. Because of this, we made sure to always keep our books in order. We also needed to be drawing salaries, which was one way to demonstrate that our business was thriving.

If our books had been a mess, the company that bought us would never have gone through with the deal. They sent an accounting company to pore over our books, going through every detail to make sure we were on the up and up with every bit of financial information we had.

By then, we'd achieved (and maintained) our goal of being the highest revenue producing, highest profit-margin health club in our county. Even when the recession hit and revenues leveled off, we'd pulled through and thrived. In the end, our finances proved that we'd achieved our fiscal goals.

Reputation. One of the key questions we were asked by the CEO of the company that bought us was, "How did you get your online review rating so high?"

Our gym was rated 4.6 out of 5 stars on major review sites. The CEO, whose company owns over 200 clubs, was very impressed by that number. When he asked how we did it, we talked with him about the strategies we've discussed throughout this book:

- Addressing an issue *before* someone has a chance to leave a bad review
- Putting our members' needs first
- Abiding by the good, old-fashioned strategy that works every time: The Golden Rule

Utilizing professional advice. We worked with a financial adviser who helped us plot out a plan for our retirement (into our nineties). We put together a wise, solid plan for setting up and using our money for decades to come. In our case, for the first eight years post-sale, we planned to still have an income, albeit a more modest income than we'd had while running the club. The idea was for us to generate a small amount of income for eight years, after which we would be able to retire fully.

If we hadn't worked with the financial advisor, we wouldn't have necessarily known how to strategize our profit from selling the club so it would extend for decades to come. We knew we were financially savvy enough not to blow through it, but still, the advisor helped us plan strategically for making our money last.

As mentioned, we'd always known we would eventually sell, but until we reached that "expand or sell" crossroads in 2018, we hadn't known exactly when it would happen. We could have gone through with the expansion, pushed through for another six or eight years, and then sold. But business was peaking, and we had negotiated a $4.2 million cash offer. At that point, our financial advisor helped us come to the decision about whether to take the offer or wait it out for another few years.

Because it was such a huge decision, we also talked with other experts to get their advice. In the end, we consulted with attorneys, accountants, and financial advisors. All advised us to sell at this time. They all had stories about business owners who waited for a better offer, and in the end, were unable to sell their businesses or had to accept a much lower offer.

It was an exciting but frightening proposition. But in the end, we settled on the adage, "a bird in the hand is worth two in the bush."

"THE PROBLEM CHILD"

When we talked with our kids about selling Christi's Fitness, we said, "What do you guys think? We really value your opinion, and we want to know."

It had always been clear to us that neither of our kids was interested in running the club. Jordan sometimes called the gym our "problem child." We had to admit she was right. Our biological children were a joy to raise but, like many a "problem child," the gym received a lot of the parents' attention.

When we talked about selling, Jordan was all for it. She said, "I think it's time to kick the third child out of the house."

We had to laugh. We knew exactly what she meant.

FINDING A BUYER AND GETTING AN OFFER

Selling a business is a daunting task, and finding the right buyer was crucial to not disrupting the service we were providing in our community. We had many interested parties who seemed like nice people but had no experience in the fitness industry. We knew that selling to such parties would be a disservice to our members, and we didn't want to do that.

The company that bought us had extensive experience running fitness clubs. That appealed to us, and when we sat down to talk with the CEO, we liked his approach and his vision for the club.

A broker negotiated the sale. The company's initial offer was to buy 49% of the company, while we retained 51% ownership. The idea was that we could run the business together. This would have been done under the condition that we'd have to use proceeds of the sale of 49% of the business to pay off our remaining debt on the property.

This offer did not appeal to us. We were given the advice that even if we retained controlling interest, chances were good that the company would pressure us to do things that went against our ideas and culture. Eventually, we were told, we were likely to get so frustrated that we'd want them to buy us out, but they'd have leverage over us. At that point, we'd likely want out so badly, we'd sell our 51% of the business for significantly less than it was worth.

The broker went back to the company and said we were not willing to do a partnership. At that point, the CEO made us an offer on an outright sale, which we accepted.

BRANDING

In the years when we were running the club, people would meet Christi and say, "Oh, there *is* a Christi." Especially toward the end, when the club was quite a bit larger, not everyone in our community realized there truly was a Christi behind Christi's Fitness.

The company that bought us had also bought many other facilities, and they've bought more since then. In the years since they took over ownership of our club, in fact, they've bought seven other clubs in Florida.

They changed the name of almost every club they bought except ours. Most likely because Christi's Fitness was so embedded in our community, there was no reason for them to change it. They said they might change it sometime in the future, but when they bought the club, they knew the name was an asset.

This was due to a couple of key factors: 1) our reputation, and 2) the fact that the club was in a small community. In a larger city, even a business with a great reputation might go through a name change after a sale, because name recognition might not mean as much in a larger area.

SALE PROCESS

We learned so much through the process of selling the business. Before we could agree on a price for the business, the land, and the building, we had to research what our actual net proceeds would be from the sale. We engaged a lawyer, an accountant, and our financial advisor to help in this process. We had to include paying off the existing debt, the broker's fee, the investor's 5%, and the capital gains tax. This was a difficult task, but so important, to avoid getting surprised by unknowns in the end.

Overall, the sales process was very smooth. Again, it was important to have professionals on our side. We would not have attempted a sale of this magnitude without a broker who understood all the ins and outs of this type of deal.

LEARNING TO LET GO

We'd expected that letting go would be bittersweet, but not difficult. After all, we were ready. We'd put in twenty-one years of blood, sweat, and tears. With a successful sale, and a clear plan forward for the next phase of our lives, we felt confident that we were, as Jordan put it, finally free of our "problem child."

But it was harder than expected, especially at first. Steve says, "In all those years, I'd come to think of the gym as a large work of art. It was a canvas that we were painting with employees, members, and a culture that we thoughtfully developed and maintained. When you work on a piece of art of that size for years and years, and then let it go, it feels like a part of you is gone, too."

Our buyer was a large, multinational company with a new CEO who was aggressively trying to turn their brand around. We sensed from him a true desire to build a strong company, with strategic long-term goals. But their systems were different than ours, and as a result, some of the long-term Christi's staffers decided to leave.

The company also utilized what they called "labor optimization"—in other words, cutting back on staff. They were more sales oriented than we'd been. Steve says, "Because we were still spending time in the club post-sale, I watched as their practices were implemented. And I learned more about number crunching and labor efficiency than I'd learned in all the years we were owners."

After the sale, both Steve and Christi continued to exercise at the club. Additionally, Christi continued to teach group exercise classes there. From force of habit, both of us would stop to place a discarded towel in a hamper, pick up trash, or move abandoned items to the lost and found.

Christi says, "A couple of members said to me, 'Oh, you're still straightening that up.' I replied, 'Yeah, it's just in me now.'"

We saw how the small things got passed over. It became clear that those were the things that were most important to members. We'd always known those little touches made the biggest difference between us and our competitors, but after we sold, when they weren't happening as often, it also became apparent how much our little touches had meant to members. It saddened us to see some of these practices abandoned.

But we've tried to let it go and focus on our own lives. We bought our house outright. We also now own a second home outright. We bought out our cars. For the first time in thirty years, we have zero debt.

The past few years, Christi has enjoyed having the opportunity to spend more time with family and help people in other contexts. She volunteers for our local hospice organization, for a Care Net Pregnancy center, and at our church. She's also taken up tennis, which she played prior to having children, but not much while we owned the club. Steve also volunteers at church and works part time at a tennis club.

THE POWER OF FRIENDSHIPS

Since selling the business, we've developed friendships with a number of people who worked with us at Christi's. It's a joy to be able to connect on a friend level with former employees. Over the years, we found that many of our staff were people with whom we would have spent more time socializing outside the club. But as we mentioned earlier, when you have an employer-employee relationship with someone, it's important to maintain professional distance. To be frank, there weren't enough hours in the day to socialize that much.

Once we no longer owned the club, this wasn't an issue. Breaking free from the employer-employee relationship allowed us to cultivate friendships that we've come to treasure in the years since we sold the business.

If we want these friendships to last, we know we have to be intentional about it. We make plans to get together for lunch or dinner, to catch up with friends. Our friendships are important, so we make a point to do that.

———

"If your actions create a legacy that inspires others to dream more, learn more, do more and become more, then, you are an excellent leader."
– Dolly Parton

———

WHAT MADE US DIFFERENT?

Over the years when we owned the club, some of our members (many of them aspiring entrepreneurs) asked us, "What makes you different? With all the clubs in town, how have you managed to make Christi's stand out the way it does?"

"When people asked me that question, I really didn't know how to answer," Steve says. "I couldn't put my finger on it. Many clubs were clean, friendly, and spent money on nice equipment, so it wasn't any of that. I think I'd usually utter something like, 'We try to sign up members that will be a good fit for our environment' or, 'We have something here for the whole family.' It wasn't until we were winding down our business that a still, small voice whispered to my soul, 'We care about them.' It was a bittersweet realization, after putting the club in new hands."

Here's the thing: when you're focused on the bottom line, caring about other people can fall to the lowest tier on your priority list. But if you run your business that way—focused exclusively on the bottom line—you're never going to stand out from your competition.

In our view, caring about people is simple. It means putting yourself in another's shoes. It's a form of loving your neighbor as yourself.

In our view, this simple adage is so powerful, it amazes us how often it's overlooked in business. In truth, it's not something that can be tracked or measured. Because there's no way to number-crunch it, a lot of business owners discount it entirely, if they consider it at all.

But we believe that true compassion is what made Christi's Fitness what it was: a highly successful business, beloved in our community. It was a place that mentored employees to become leaders, put the customer before the dollar, and that we were proud to call our own.

When genuine kindness connects people, it's transformational. And when your business does that, you're not just running a company. You're creating a legacy—together.

ELEVATE THE ORDINARY

- Keeping your books in order is essential for obtaining financing, knowing your true profit margin and being prepared to sell if the opportunity arises. What bookkeeping practices and reporting can you put in place to ensure you are seeing accurate financials?
- As early as possible in running your business, define your long-term plans and goals.
- Be aware that your plan will likely evolve over time. Understand the essence of your plan, and as things change in the course of running your business, strive to maintain a balance between flexibility and goals achievement.
- Understand that how you treat people—including employees, customers, and those in your wider community—defines

your business more than any product you sell or service you provide ever could.

- Run your business using the simple adage of the Golden Rule.

CHRISTI'S FITNESS EMPLOYEE HANDBOOK

christi's

F I T N E S S

be inspired

Welcome to Christi's Fitness! We know you'll enjoy being part of our staff. We believe our staff is the true strength of our business. We strive to provide a work environment where you can enjoy what you do, work as a team, and have opportunity to grow within the organization.

This manual is to help you understand our purpose and practices as you begin your work with us. The policies and procedures outlined help us provide professional service to our members and protect the culture that has made Christi's Fitness a great place to earn a living and grow as a person.

OUR VISION:

To set the fitness industry standards for safety, customer service, education and lifestyle enhancement for adult and children's fitness programs. To provide staff, members, and students an environment based on biblical values that promote their growth physically, emotionally, intellectually, and spiritually.

MISSION STATEMENT:

To make the fitness experience an inspiration for the families of our community.

CORE PURPOSE:

To make a positive difference in the life of everyone who comes into our facility.

COMPANY CULTURE:

- Smiling, positive, and friendly
- Safe and well maintained

- Eager to help and listen
- Clean
- Knowledgeable and informed
- Innovative
- Welcoming, non-intimidating environment
- Make our customers feel special
- Responsive and consistent with customer service
- Fair with conflict resolution

CORE VALUES:

- All staff, members, and students will be held accountable to be considerate, polite, understanding, forgiving and unbiased to all races.
- The staff will complete any necessary training and education to safely and effectively lead members and students to their fitness goals.
- We will provide more than what is expected for our members and students even when it is difficult.
- We will always reach out to someone in need to try to provide appropriate assistance.
- We will provide our employees an exciting, uplifting work environment with opportunities for growth and reward.
- We will never focus on money more than people.
- We will remain positive and compassionate even when dealing with adversity.

DRESS CODE:

You are allotted one uniform shirt for each day that you work per week. Shirts will be different for each department. All other shirts may be purchased at cost. There is a list of prices at the Welcome Desk. Please give your name and size to your Department Head. Employees working less than the 90-day probationary period will be charged $10 for each shirt they were given.

- Hats are not allowed except for swim instructors who are given a Christi's Fitness visor.
- Sneakers or shoes must appear clean.

WELCOME DESK:

- Christi's shirt
- Black, khaki, white or jean shorts
- Capris or Jeans (no holes)
- No yoga pants

GYMNASTICS, MOMMY & ME & BIRTHDAY PARTY STAFF:

- Christi's shirt
- Athletic shorts, pants
- Sneakers or barefoot while coaching/teaching
- No jeans

KIDS' KINGDOM:

- Christi's shirt
- Jeans, capris, or nice shorts

GROUP EXERCISE & MARTIAL ARTS INSTRUCTORS:

- Attire fitting to discipline

DANCE INSTRUCTORS:

- Studio C Dance Shirt
- Capris, shorts, athletic pants
- Barefoot or dance shoes

PERSONAL TRAINERS:

- Personal Trainer shirt/polo
- Athletic shorts/pants
- Sneakers

PHONE USE / TEXTING:

- Cell phones should be turned on silent and set aside while you are working.

TIME CLOCK:

Staff members must clock in and out at the reception computer themselves using their 4-digit user ID number. The use of that number is limited to the person it represents. Use of that number by someone else is grounds for termination. The password is set up with the Human Resource Director.

If you forget to clock in or out, leave a note for Office Manager or Administrative Assistant with your full name, date and time of the punch you missed.

BREAKS & EATING:

Any employee working a shift of 3 consecutive hours will be allowed a 15 minute (paid) break to eat. Any employee working a shift of 6 consecutive hours will be allowed a 30 minute (paid) break to eat. Drinks and snacks only at the Welcome Desk. Full meals are to be eaten in the office. If you are leaving the building to get food, this is considered part of your paid break time.

CONDUCT:

- Always smile and be friendly to the members while working out.
- If a member asks you a question during a workout, please try to help them briefly. You may want to get another staff member that is working if the issue calls for it.
- When taking a class, if the class is full, it is your responsibility to make room for a member. For example, getting off your bike in spin, or giving up your step, etc.
- When working out in the weight room, you must wear something that covers your mid-section.
- Trainers and staff may not "reserve" or "hold" cardio equipment in the weight room, for interval training, etc.
- If you see or hear anything that is in violation of our weight room guidelines (posted in the weight room) please report to Steve or Christi.
- During the busy season (Jan.-Apr.) you may be asked to avoid certain busy times of day in the weight room.

These rules come from member suggestions, comments and our years of experience in the health club industry. You, as a staff member, have the privilege to use the facility as often as you want. You also have the responsibility to make sure the members come first and to represent the club, on or off the clock, to the standards we have set forth.

Christi's Fitness has developed a great reputation in the community, due largely to our great staff! That's you!

PLEASE REFRAIN FROM ALL OF THESE INAPPROPRIATE BEHAVIORS:

- Shouting (unless you are instructing a group)
- Profanity
- Disrespectful or rude comments
- Gossip
- Verbal and non-verbal personal attacks
- Sexual remarks or overtones
- Commenting negatively about someone else
- Physical or mental abuse
- Racial, ethnic, or sexual insults, jokes or slurs
- Sexual harassment
- Verbal or physical sexual advances
- Sexually explicit statements

NEW EMPLOYEE TRAINING
WELCOME DESK TRAINING:

You will receive training with another front desk employee & your supervisor before you will be by yourself at the front desk. You will learn the basics of checking members in, answering the phone, ringing up sales, and washing and folding towels. Learning member sign-up procedure will be done with some welcome desk employees as well as the Welcome Desk Manager. Every Welcome Desk employee will be required to observe and participate in select adult and children's classes and services during the training process. You will receive a checklist of the classes/programs to observe. Once the list is complete, you will submit it to the Welcome Desk Manager to be paid for the 10 hours it takes to complete the orientation. This will familiarize you with the club and prepare you to describe the various programs we offer. You will be required to attend a monthly meeting the last Wednesday of every month at 12:00pm in the main office.

GYMNASTICS & PRE-SCHOOL TRAINING GUIDELINES:

You will meet with the supervisor to go through general class formats, room safety, and move-up sheets. Then you will spend 1-3 weeks for two to three hours at a time in scheduled classes alongside any other instructor. The first week will be in observation and the following weeks you will participate. There will be scheduled ongoing training sessions to focus on specific areas of need that all instructors will attend.

MOMMY & ME TRAINING:

You will meet with the supervisor for 1 hour to go over the Mommy & Me class format, safety procedures and where everything is located. You will train for 5 classes shadowing different instructors and leading portions of the class. After a month, you will be ready to lead your own class and the director will shadow your class.

BIRTHDAY PARTY TRAINING:

You will meet with the supervisor to go through room safety, room set up, birthday party format, and where all products are kept for birthday parties. The supervisor will also go over your availability for birthday parties on Saturdays (10am-5pm) and/or Sundays (12:30-5:30pm).

DANCE TRAINING:

You will meet with the supervisor to go through specifics in reference to the Christi's Dance program guidelines and expectations. You'll then be scheduled to observe some of the dance classes.

PERSONAL TRAINER TRAINING:

You'll meet one on one with your supervisor to go through all of the requirements and paperwork for the personal trainers. You will need to show proof of national certification, current CPR, and proof of liability insurance at this time. You will lead a supervisor through a mock workout on the equipment.

GROUP EXERCISE INSTRUCTOR TRAINING:

You will be required to demonstrate a class to a supervisor where they will ask questions along the way. You'll then do a class for our members while the supervisor takes the class to observe.

CHILDREN'S SWIM INSTRUCTOR TRAINING:

Pre-hiring – Meet with the Swim Administrator/Head Coach to go over the swim program and observe 2 swim classes. An in-water evaluation will be scheduled with the Head Coach.

4 hours of water training, in-water assisting/shadowing, video training, CPR certification, monthly coaches meeting, ongoing season training. A review will be held after 30 days.

KIDS' KINGDOM TRAINING:

You will meet with your supervisor to go through check in and check out policy in the Kingdom, incident reports, safety and where everything is located. Then you will work a shift as an extra person mainly to observe and ask questions. There will be scheduled meetings every other month that you will be required to attend.

REQUEST FOR TIME OFF:

You are responsible for finding a substitute if you will be gone. After you have secured your replacement, contact the director of your department to inform them of your time off. In case of a personal emergency, you must contact the appropriate program director to inform them of your situation.

PAY PERIOD:

The pay period is every two weeks starting on a Tuesday and ending on a Monday. Direct Deposit will be used for your payroll. The password to receive email pay stubs is the **first four letters of your last name and the last four digits of your social security number (no capitals or spaces needed).**

RAISES/REVIEWS:

Your initial employment is a 90-day probationary period. If, for any reason, your performance is deemed to be unsatisfactory during the first 90 days, your employment will be terminated. Reviews for potential raises are done annually, after your 90-day period, with your supervisor.

KIDS' KINGDOM (KK) EMPLOYEE USE:

1. Department Heads should inform the KK Director anytime they hire new staff that will be using KK.

2. If the new staff member comes to the club to exercise themselves, they need to follow KK rules as they are set up for all members, with a 2-hour maximum time limit.

3. If you are working a shift at the facility, you may use KK during that period. If the shift is over 2 hours, you must take your children out for a short break / snack. The KK workers are unable to feed them in KK and your children need a break from the room.

4. The exception to the above is if your child is struggling to stay in the room or is being very difficult for the staff to handle, then you will be asked to make other arrangements for a period before trying to use it again.

4. This is a benefit and a privilege to our staff, please be considerate of the KK staff as we are NOT set up to be a daycare facility and parents must be on site at all times when their children are in KK.

POOL SAFETY:

There are NO lifeguards on duty. Members swim at their own risk. There are signs posted.

NO children are allowed in the pool unless attending a private swim lesson with a Christi's Instructor, participating in a scheduled swim class or during family swim time.

GYMNASTICS ROOM SAFETY GUIDELINES:

- No adults are allowed in the room except with Mommy & Me classes, parent of a birthday child during the party to take pictures, or during an adult fitness class using the gymnastics room floor.
- No adult members are allowed on the gymnastics equipment unless they are with a personal trainer or a gymnastics coach is present.
- No children are allowed in the room without an instructor present.
- While coaches are instructing, their own children may NOT be on the equipment if not in an organized class.
- Instructors need to position themselves at all times to be able to see their entire group.
- When jumping into the pit the student must enter feet first or bottom first.
- If someone is injured in the pit, the instructor should have everyone stay in the pit so as to not move the foam around. The instructor should not jump into the pit. The supervisor will handle the situation according to our emergency response guidelines.

WEIGHT ROOM ETIQUETTE:

We allow you to work out on your own time, respecting the following:

- Please allow members to "work in" if you notice they are waiting for a piece of strength equipment you are on.
- Do not take the last piece of cardio equipment during a peak time.

- Please wait until there are at least two pieces of cardio equipment available before taking one.
- If the cardio equipment fills up while you are on a piece, please get off to open up one for the next member. Members will often leave the club if the cardio equipment is full.

EMERGENCY PROCEDURES:

Where things are located:
- The AED is located in the weight room between the locker room doors.
- <u>First Aid Kits and *Emergency Procedures* notebooks are located throughout the facility:</u> Behind the welcome desk, in the cabinet next to the pool, in the gymnastics room on the filing cabinet immediately to your left when you walk through the doors, in the nursery and in the Studio C office.
- There is a CPR mask in the AED enclosure.
- Ice packs are located in the freezer in the main office, in the gymnastics room and in the Studio C office.
- Name, address, phone number to the facility are on the front of all *Emergency Procedures* notebooks.
- Incident reports are located in the front cover of all *Emergency Procedures* notebooks.

ACCIDENT REPORTS:

All accidents that occur MUST have an accident report filled out, no matter how minor.

An accident report needs to be filled out by a staff member. The injured person does NOT have to fill out a report; if the injury occurs to a child, the parent needs to sign a form informing them of the incident report. Please get any injured adult to sign the incident report.

Both reports MUST be put into Christi or Steve's box at the front desk on the day that it happened, and send a text to them that it is there.

Only facts should be recorded on the accident report – not your emotions or opinions of the situation.

Remember never to admit fault but be sensitive and caring. You can say, "I'm sorry this happened."

The owners or directors will make a follow-up phone call and handle any insurance-related questions.

WHEN CALLING 911:

1. Take down the AED that is located in the weight room between the two locker room doors if the issue involves fainting or the person has stopped breathing.

2. A staff member should always stay with an injured person while telling someone else to call 911. Always direct one person – "Tom please call 911." They will need to know the club address. 911 will question the caller and set the response in motion.

3. Have another staff person keeping bystanders out of the way. A staff person should always be at the door to greet the emergency response team and direct them to the emergency.

4. If someone has had a minor fall or injury, send someone to get the first aid kit and the *Emergency Procedures* notebook. Follow the guidelines outlined in the book.

CHRISTI'S FITNESS DEPARTMENT HEADS (10/26/17)

Owner: Steve Wade

Owner & Group Exercise Director: Christi Wade

ADMINISTRATIVE STAFF/MANAGEMENT

Studio C Manager: Dadra Smith

Welcome Desk Manager: Tisha Lowery

Assistant Welcome Desk Manager: Kyle Yencho

General Manager: Don Weston

Graphic Design: Nick Ellis

Insurance Memberships/Healthways: Nancy Depp

Office Manager: Noelle Weston

Maintenance Manager: Dan LaBelle

PROGRAM DEPARTMENT HEADS

Birthday Party Staff Administrator: Eva Platenburg

Children's Aqua Administrator: Dadra Smith

Children's Dance & Performing Arts: Ashly Billé

Gymnastics Program: Randi Murdough

Kids' Kingdom: Allie Alto

Mommy & Me & Preschool Gymnastics: Hannah Cleversey

GM, Personal Training Director/Tribe Director: Don Weston

BUSINESS PARTNERS

Acupuncture: Dana Gulati

Martial Arts: Jason Wesley

Massage: Jason Goss

Plank Pilates Studio: Rachel Clark

Weston Speed Academy: Don Weston

Afterword

It's important to note the writing of this book took place before and during the COVID-19 global pandemic that hit the United States. Health clubs as well as other businesses were forced to close for months. The federal government provided some financial aid for payroll and utilities, but many businesses suffered.

When faced with a fire, hurricanes, new competition, a recession or even a pandemic, it's difficult to navigate if you haven't been building a culture of trust, innovation and change beforehand. These things can help you recover from the unexpected. It's when things are going smoothly that we need to be preparing for the worst. Bringing your staff together regularly and connecting with members will build a defense system for the battles you can't see coming.

The title of this book was written before the pandemic surfaced. The phrase "We're in this together" has become popular as we unite to get through the worst health crisis this nation has ever seen.

The better our relationships are before the next disaster strikes, the more we can lean on each other and pull together to get through it. We hope this book can be an inspiration for entrepreneurs and others to that end.

Acknowledgements

We have had the ability to employ close to a thousand people through our 21 years in business. Many have contributed, supported, and served the residents of Vero Beach with generous and caring hearts. They not only made an imprint on the members but also on us, we could not have done it without them, and we thank you from the bottom of our hearts. We had an amazing TEAM!

Here are a few that helped us build trust and support in our community by putting children first. Yes, this is some of our staff that helped nurture, guide and train the kiddos! We love you and honor you for that dedication: Allie Alto, Jennifer Ballester, Monica Bauer, Brittany Beliveau, Bailey Bellefleur, Ashly Bille, Kelly Buckes, Brian Califf, Kelly Camacho, Amanda Chylack, Andrea Cortez, Jill Davis, Carol Dubon, Karen Freeman , Kimberly Gardner, Lara Gormley, Jeff Gothard, Celeste Howder, Tracey Kea, Jen Jenkins Leiti, Neddie Masculino–Dewey, Connie McCord, Carey McDivitt, Olivia McManus, Kim Mead, Peggy Moore, Terra Mundy, Crystal Nickell, Jennifer Patty, Katie Peavely, Lydia Pittman, Eva Plantenberg, Heather Reeb, Jocelyn Sample, Angie Schepers, Whitney Schroeder, Linda Simos, Lynn Sonier, Jill Toohey, Wendy Vander Sys, Emily Waage, Jason Wesley, Melissa Williams.

Thank you to many of our competitive team gymnasts that came back through the years and worked for us. What beautiful examples of dedication, strong work ethics and commitment, you all showed! And the children loved that you could demonstrate almost everything. Hannah Borchardt, The Cleversey sisters (Hannah, Jessica & Christina), Kristin Coxson, Victoria Damutz, Taylor & Tessa DeLange, McKenzie Flinchum, Kristin Gordon, Samantha Grimm, Alex Hagood, Ashley Hinson, Maggie Liott, Kendall & Kaley Loewendick, Molly Metcalf, Elizabeth Nelson, Emily Nelson, Emma & Leah Rodriguez, Katie Sonier, Caityln Taylor, Emily Thomas, Maia Tinder, Lauren Velde, Grace & Abby Waage, Madison Ware, Grayson Welchel, Kysa Wetmiller.

Thank you to all those who worked with our adult membership whether instructing, training, organizing events, administrating, marketing, maintenance, etc....your professionalism, willingness to put the member first, gave us a staff that members wanted to be around & who they could trust. We loved that many of you were open to anything and wore many hats at the club. Dawn Bamberg ,Brian Bedard, Heather Rae Bennett, Erin Bevard, Trish Boddy, Jennifer Brandt, DeAnna Burns, John Campbell, Daniel Campbell, Pat Carroll, Abbe Chane, Julie Cielo, Rachel Clark, Emily Colontrelle, Angela Combs, Pamela DeChellis, Nancy Depp, Nick Ellis, Michele Falls, Gwen Flynn, Marcia Garrett, Janie Gianoulis, Jason Goss, Linda Graham, Lewis Grove, Mary Margaret Hatch, Leah Hellemann, Chris Holly, Jim Huff, Courtney Jones, Lorie Ann Kovaleski, Dan LaBelle, Missy Liott, Lori Long, Tisha Lowery, Mary Lunn, Melissa Matakaetis, Pam Mitchell, Cara & Jason Noel, Veronique Ory Sturiale, Jera Payton Torres, Christine Purdy, Marsea Purdy, Natalie Rancourt, Beth Ratliff, Jose Ratto, Mary Replogle, Edwin Rivera, Jen Robbins, Jenny Roberts, Gerianne

Robinson, Katie Rosario, Rebecca Schlitt, Karen Shick, Barbara Shugrue, Shannon Sims, Dadra Smith, Stephanie Smith, Jake Sonzogni, Amanda Steadman, Lori Strazzulla, Lorraine Sutherland, Peggy Sutliff, Kim Thornton, Ron Toperzer, Danny Trennepohl, Angie Watson, Don & Noelle Weston, Jill Wheeler, Geleene Wilke, Lenore Wolaver, Shelly Yeager, Kyle Yencho, Bonnie Zorc.

Thanks to Mike & Laura Bagby, Tracey Russell and Pastor Greg Sempsrott for your friendship and support through the tough times. Your ability to speak the truth, in love, has helped us deepen our faith and stay together.

Thank you to our parents: John & Lenore, Bill & Iris for the foundation you help set, laying the ground work for our values and faith, your wisdom and guidance through the years and your constant love. To our siblings, Carol, Billy, Susan, Nancy, Mark and Karla for your love and support as well as advice when we need it. To our children, Jordan and Brenton (as well as his wife Andi), we are so grateful and blessed to have you in our lives. YOU inspire us!

Thank you, Lord God, above all for being our savior, father, and friend through it all. For it is You, God who has the master plan and keeps it all together.

Made in the USA
Columbia, SC
13 February 2021